Digital Defense:
The Essential Guide for Cyber Security

Selim VARIŞLI

TABLE OF CONTENTS

Introduction

The rapid growth of the internet and its widespread use has changed the way we communicate, work and conduct business. The internet has become a critical component of our daily lives and we rely on it to perform a variety of tasks such as online banking, shopping, communication and information sharing. However, the increasing use of the internet has also led to a rise in the number of security threats that can compromise our privacy and safety.

Internet security refers to the measures and techniques used to protect online systems, including networks, servers and individual devices from cyber attacks and other security threats. These security measures aim to protect sensitive information, such as financial data, personal information and intellectual property from unauthorized access, theft or damage.

Internet security is constantly evolving and cybercriminals are always finding new ways to exploit vulnerabilities in online systems. This is why it is essential to stay informed about the latest security threats and to adopt appropriate measures to protect yourself from them. It's a critical concern for anyone who uses the internet. By staying informed about the latest security threats and taking measures, you can keep your sensitive information secure and online activities safe.

There are several reasons why internet security is important:

Protecting Sensitive Information: The internet is used to store and transmit a vast amount of sensitive information, including financial data, personal information and intellectual property. If this information is compromised, it can lead to significant financial losses, damage to reputation and loss of privacy.

Preventing Cyber Attacks: The internet is a prime target for cyber attacks, including hacking, malware, phishing and ransomware attacks. These attacks can cause significant damage to systems and networks, disrupt operations and steal sensitive information.

Maintaining Business Continuity: Businesses rely on the internet for communication, collaboration and operations. If a cyber attack results in the disruption of online systems, it can have a significant impact on business operations and result in serious financial losses.

Ensuring Compliance: Many industries and governments have regulations and laws that require organizations to protect sensitive information and secure their systems. Failure to comply with these regulations can result in significant fines and damage to reputation.

Protecting National Security: The internet is critical to national security, as it is used to support military operations, intelligence gathering and critical infrastructure. Protecting online systems is essential to maintaining national security.

How people's online habits must change in time because of cybercrimes?

In the past few decades, cyber crime and attacks have become a significant issue. As a result, it has become increasingly important for people to become more vigilant about their online habits and protect themselves from potential cyber threats.

The first and most important step people should take when it comes to protecting themselves online is to set up strong passwords and two-factor authentication on all of their accounts. Strong passwords are extremely important as they provide an extra layer of security against potential threats. It's essential to use a different password for each online account and to use a mix of upper and lowercase letters, numbers and special characters. Many people still use weak passwords or use the same password across multiple platforms. Implementing strong and unique passwords combined with two-factor authentication can significantly enhance security. Two-factor authentication is especially important as it further secures an account and makes it difficult for malicious actors to gain access.

Another important step people should take is to be aware of phishing scams. Phishing is when someone attempts to gain access to confidential information or account details by sending an email that looks like it is from a legitimate source. If the person receiving the email is not careful, they may provide the malicious actor with their information. It is therefore important to be aware of phishing scams and not click on any links in emails that look suspicious.

People should also be careful about what information they share online. From social media profiles to banking information, it is important to limit the amount of personal data that is shared on the internet. This is because hackers or malicious actors could access this information which could lead to fraudulent activity or identity theft. With the increasing use of internet, it's more important than ever to be mindful of what information you share online. The internet can be a powerful tool for connecting people and exchanging information but it can also be a dangerous place where personal information can be easily misused.

Social media platforms offer a unique space to connect with friends and family but they can also expose you to serious risks. Posting personal information, such as your full name, address or birthdate, might seem harmless to share with friends but it can be a goldmine for cybercriminals looking to perpetrate identity theft or other malicious activities.

It's also a good idea to regularly review privacy settings on all online accounts to ensure that sharing only the information wanted to share. Most online services offer privacy settings that allow users to control who can access their information and how much is visible to the public. Familiarize yourself with these settings and ensure that you configure them according to your comfort level. Being careful with what information shared online can help protect users identity and prevent fraudulent activities.

Oversharing on social media can attract unwanted attention from cyberstalkers. Publishing too many details about your daily routine or travel plans could make you vulnerable to physical harm or burglary. It's crucial to maintain a balance between staying connected and safeguarding your privacy.

Many websites and mobile apps collect user data for various purposes, often without full awareness of user. Be cautious when granting permissions to third-party apps as they may gain access to sensitive information, leading to potential data breaches or misuse.

There's a definition called digital footprint. It refers to the traces of information you leave behind while engaging online. It includes your social media activity, online purchases, search history and much more. Though seemingly innocuous, this information can be pieced together by malicious actors to create a comprehensive profile of your identity, preferences and habits.

A cumulation of psychological manipulation tactics called social engineering used by cybercriminals to trick individuals into divulging sensitive information or performing specific actions. Phishing is one common form of social engineering, wherein fraudulent emails, messages or websites impersonate legitimate entities to extract personal data, login credentials or financial information. Identifying phishing attempts can be challenging as attackers have become adept at crafting convincing messages. Nevertheless, learning to spot red flags such as suspicious URLs, poor grammar and unexpected requests for personal information can be crucial in thwarting phishing attacks.

Users should be wary of malicious websites. Websites that are designed to appear legitimate but are actually malicious are known as "spoofing sites" created by hackers to steal your personal information or infect your computer with malwares. These sites are often using logos, fonts and colors that are similar to the real site. They can be very convincing and it can be difficult to tell the difference between a spoofing site and the real one. Once you enter your personal information on a spoofing site, the hackers can use it to steal your identity or access your financial accounts.

In addition to being cautious when browsing the internet, it's important to keep your computer up to date with the latest security patches and updates. This can help to prevent vulnerabilities that could be exploited by cybercriminals. You should also use strong and unique passwords for all of your online accounts and enable two-factor authentication where possible.

If you do suspect that you've been the victim of a cyber attack or that your personal information has been compromised, it's important to act quickly. You should contact your bank to report any suspicious activity and change your passwords for all of your accounts.

Users also should be aware of the potential dangers of public Wi-Fi networks. They are available almost everywhere in these days but they are not secure and can be accessed by anyone on the same network. This means that any information sent over a public Wi-Fi network is vulnerable to malicious actors. Hackers can easily intercept sensitive information such as passwords, credit card numbers and other personal data, leaving users open to identity theft and fraud. Therefore, it is essential to avoid accessing sensitive information such as online banking and shopping on public Wi-Fi networks.

Another way to protect oneself while using public Wi-Fi is to use a virtual private network (VPN). A VPN is a service that creates a secure and encrypted connection between the user's device and the internet. VPNs are widely available and many are free to use. By using a VPN, users can keep their online activities private and secure, even when using public Wi-Fi networks. VPNs are an effective way to protect oneself from cyber-attacks and identity theft while using public Wi-Fi networks.

Cybersecurity threats are not limited to individuals but also affect businesses and organizations. Businesses and organizations must implement effective cyber security measures to protect their networks, sensitive data and customers' personal information. This includes using firewalls, anti-virus software, intrusion detection and prevention systems and other security measures to detect and prevent cyber-attacks.

It is becoming increasingly important for users to be aware of their online habits as cybercrimes have become more common. Cyber security is an essential aspect of modern life. With the increasing reliance on technology, the risks associated with cyber attacks continue to grow. By taking the necessary precautions, staying informed about the latest trends and threats and adopting emerging technologies, we can protect ourselves and our sensitive information from cyber threats. The future of cyber security is promising and it is up to us to stay ahead of the curve and ensure that our digital lives remain safe and secure.

--- o ---

This book is divided into several chapters that cover the essential concepts and technologies related to internet security. The chapters are organized in a logical order, building upon each other to provide a comprehensive understanding of the topic. The following is a brief summary of each chapter.

Chapter I: Network Security

Network security is the practice of defending networks from malicious activity, such as unauthorized access, disruption and modification. It includes the processes and technologies used to secure the network infrastructure, such as routers, firewalls and intrusion detection systems. A secure network should be designed and implemented to ensure confidentiality, integrity, availability and accountability of the data that is transmitted over the network.

Chapter II: Web Security

Email security is the process of protecting emails from malicious activities, such as spam, phishing, malware and other cyber threats. It involves the use of various tools and technologies, such as encryption, authentication and anti-malware software, to ensure that emails are secure and can only be accessed by authorized users.

Chapter III: Email Security

In this chapter, we examine the key concepts and technologies related to email security. We discuss the different types of email attacks, the components of a secure email infrastructure and the best practices for securing email systems.

Chapter IV: Data Security

Data security is the practice of protecting data from unauthorized access or loss. It involves the use of various tools and technologies, such as encryption, authentication and access control to protect data from malicious attacks. Data security also involves the implementation of policies and procedures to ensure that the data remains secure and only accessible to authorized users.

Chapter V: Cloud Security

Cloud security is essential in protecting data and applications that are hosted on cloud computing platforms. The components of a secure cloud infrastructure include authentication, authorization and encryption technologies, as well as access control, intrusion detection and activity logging. These components work together to provide a robust layer of security that can help protect against malicious attacks. Without proper security measures in place organizations can be vulnerable to malicious attacks, data breaches and data theft. One of the most important aspects of cloud security is understanding the different types of cloud attacks. These can range from malicious insiders to denial-of-service attacks and it's important to be aware of the different threats when designing a secure cloud infrastructure. By understanding the different types of cloud attacks and the components of a secure cloud infrastructure organizations can ensure that their cloud-based systems are protected from malicious attacks.

Chapter VI: Mobile Device Security

The advancement of mobile technology has revolutionized the way we communicate and interact with the world around us. However, with this convenience and access to data comes the threat of cyberattacks and malicious actors looking to exploit security vulnerabilities. Mobile device security is a critical topic in the modern age. As the use of mobile devices continues to grow, so does the risk of malicious attacks. To protect mobile devices from these threats, it is important to understand the different types of mobile device attacks, the components of a secure mobile infrastructure and the best practices for securing mobile devices. We will look at the basics of security protocols, encryption and authentication, as well as the more advanced topics of malware detection, privacy regulations and risk management strategies.

Chapter VII: Endpoint Security

Endpoint security is designed to protect the endpoint devices (such as laptops, tablets and mobile phones) of an organization from malicious attacks. By utilizing a combination of hardware and software technologies organizations can secure their endpoint devices from external threats like malware, viruses and other malicious actors. Endpoint security is especially important in today's digital world, as the number of devices connected to the internet is constantly growing. With more devices comes an increased risk of attacks, which is why it is essential for organizations to have a comprehensive endpoint security solution in place. Endpoint security solutions should include both proactive and reactive measures to protect against malicious threats. Proactive measures include patching and antivirus software, while reactive measures include intrusion detection and user authentication. We will examine the different aspects of endpoint security, including the technologies used to protect endpoint devices, how to deploy them and how to monitor their effectiveness.

Chapter VIII: Identity and Access Management (IAM)

IAM is a critical component of cyber security, as it provides a secure way to manage user accounts and access to digital resources. IAM systems allow administrators to set up and maintain control over the authentication, authorization and access control of users and digital resources. IAM enables organizations to protect their digital resources from unauthorized access, while also ensuring that authorized users can access the resources they need. IAM systems generally include user authentication and authorization, password policies, identity and access management systems, user access management, single sign-on (SSO) and more. User authentication and authorization ensure that only authorized users can access digital resources, while password policies set the rules and guidelines for user passwords. We will discuss the importance of IAM, the various components of IAM systems and the best practices for using them.

Chapter IX: Cryptography

Cryptography is used to protect sensitive data from unauthorized access, as well as for verifying the integrity of data. Cryptography is the art and science of transforming plaintext into unreadable coding, known as ciphertext. This effectively prevents anyone from understanding the data without a decryption key. Cryptography is used to protect data in transit, stored in databases or stored on physical media. In addition, cryptography is also used to authenticate users, create digital signatures and ensure secure communication between two parties. Cryptography is an ever-evolving field as new technologies and algorithms are regularly developed, allowing for more secure forms of encryption. We will explore the fundamentals of cryptography and the use cases of cryptography in the cybersecurity space.

Chapter X: Incident Response and Management

Incident response and management is an essential component of any cyber security strategy. The purpose of incident response and management is to provide a clear and organized way to detect, respond to and mitigate any cybersecurity incident, breaches or threats. Incident response and management involves the identification, containment and eradication of these threats, as well as the investigation and analysis of the causes of the incident or threat. It also includes the development of various policies and procedures to ensure that any security incident is handled correctly and efficiently. We will examine the fundamentals of incident response and management and provide an overview of the various processes and procedures required to effectively respond to and manage any cybersecurity incident.

Chapter XI: Understanding Social Engineering

When it comes to cyber security, one of the most insidious and potent threats faced by organizations is social engineering. Unlike traditional hacking methods that rely on exploiting technical vulnerabilities, social engineering exploits the vulnerabilities of human psychology and trust. In this chapter, we'll try to understand the intricate world of social engineering, various techniques, real-world examples, the psychology behind it, the methods to defend against it and the psychological approach cybercriminals use to manipulate their targets.

Chapter XII: Answers To Common Questions

In addition to specific topic headings related to cyber security, we will answer questions about simple security measures that are frequently encountered in daily life and common questions about cyber security in this section.

Chapter XIII: The Future Of Cybersecurity

As technology continues to evolve, the threat landscape of the internet is constantly changing. Staying ahead of these threats and understanding the future trends in internet security is essential for organizations to effectively protect their digital assets. In this chapter, we will discuss some of the most significant future trends in internet security that are expected to shape the field in the years to come.

I. NETWORK SECURITY

A. Overview

Internet has become a critical component of modern life. As a result, network security has become increasingly important to ensure that sensitive information is protected, cyber attacks are prevented and the integrity of connected systems is maintained. In this chapter, we provide an overview of network security and the key concepts and technologies that are used to secure online systems.

Network security is an important part of any cybersecurity strategy, as malicious actors often target networks in order to gain access to sensitive data or systems. Network security is the practice of protecting networks and network accessible resources from unauthorized access, misuse or disruption. There are a variety of methods used to ensure network security, including firewalls, encryption, access control and other security measures.

Network security involves several different components, including physical security, authentication and authorization. Physical security refers to the protection of the equipment and infrastructure that form a network. This includes physical access control, preventing tampering and damage, as well as environmental control such as temperature and humidity. Authentication is the process of verifying the identity of a user or system, often through the use of passwords or encryption keys. Authorization is the process of granting permission or access to a user or system.

Firewalls are an important part of network security. Firewalls act as a barrier between a network and the outside world, blocking malicious actors from gaining access. Firewalls can be either hardware or software based and can be configured to block certain types of traffic or deny access, based on user roles.

Encryption is another important part of network security. Encryption is the process of transforming data into an unintelligible form that can only be decrypted with a specific key. It is used to protect sensitive data from being accessed by unauthorised users. Network security also involves the use of access control systems, which are used to restrict access to certain network resources.

Finally, network security also involves managing and monitoring network traffic. This can be done through the use of intrusion detection systems, which are used to detect suspicious or malicious traffic. Network security also involves implementing security policies that define how users interact with the network, as well as how data is handled and stored on the network.

A secure network must include several key components to ensure that sensitive information is protected and cyber attacks are prevented. Some of the key components of a secure network include:

Firewalls: Firewalls are devices or software programs that act as a barrier between a network and the internet, controlling incoming and outgoing traffic.

Virtual Private Networks (VPN): VPNs allow remote users to securely connect to a network over the internet.

Intrusion Detection and Prevention Systems (IDPS): IDPSs are systems that detect and prevent unauthorized access to a network.

Antivirus and Anti-Malware Software: Antivirus and anti-malware software is used to detect and remove malicious softwares.

In addition to using the components of a secure network, it is also important to implement best practices for securing online systems. Some of the best practices include:

Regularly updating software: Regularly updating software, including operating systems and applications, is critical to ensure that vulnerabilities are patched.

Implementing strong passwords: Strong passwords help to prevent unauthorized access to online systems.

Regularly backing up data: Regularly backing up data helps to ensure that sensitive information is protected in the event of a data loss.

Monitoring network traffic: Monitoring network traffic can help to detect potential security threats and prevent cyber attacks.

Network security is critical to ensure that sensitive information is protected, cyber attacks are prevented and the integrity of online systems is maintained. This chapter provides an overview of the key concepts and technologies that are used to secure online systems, including the different types of network attacks, the components of a secure network and the best practices for securing online systems. The following chapters explains the details of each topic to provide a more thorough understanding of network security.

B. Types of Network Attacks and How They Work

Network security is critical to prevent a wide range of attacks that can target online systems. This chapter is an overview of the most common types of network attacks. Understanding the different types of network attacks and how they work is important to ensure that systems and networks can be secured against potential threats.

B.1.   Denial of Service (DoS) Attacks

Denial of Service (DoS) attacks aim to overload a network or system with traffic, making it unavailable to users. DoS attacks can be achieved through a variety of methods, including:

Flooding: Flooding involves sending a large volume of traffic to a network or system, overwhelming it and making it unavailable to users.

Amplification Attacks: Amplification attacks involve using a third-party system to increase the volume of traffic sent to a target system, making it unavailable.

Distributed Denial-of-Service (DDoS) Attacks: DDoS attacks involve coordinating a large number of systems to simultaneously attack a target, making it unavailable.

B.2.   Man-in-the-Middle (MitM) Attacks

Man-in-the-Middle (MitM) attacks involve an attacker intercepting and manipulating communications between two systems. MitM attacks can occur in a variety of ways, including:

ARP Spoofing: ARP spoofing involves an attacker intercepting and altering ARP (Address Resolution Protocol) messages to redirect traffic to their own system.

SSL Stripping: SSL stripping involves removing encryption from secure communications, allowing an attacker to intercept and manipulate communications.

B.3.   Packet Sniffing

Packet sniffing involves capturing and analyzing network traffic to gather sensitive information. Packet sniffing can be performed through a variety of methods, including:

Promiscuous Mode: Promiscuous mode involves putting a network interface into a mode that allows it to capture all traffic, even if it is not intended for that system.

ARP Spoofing: ARP spoofing can also be used for packet sniffing, by redirecting traffic to an attacker's system.

B.4.   Malware

Malware is malicious software that can be used to compromise online systems. Malware can be spread through a variety of methods, including:
Phishing Emails: Phishing emails are emails that contain malicious links or attachments, which can infect systems when opened.

Drive-by Downloads: Drive-by downloads involve infecting systems with malware through a web browser, without the user's knowledge or consent.

C. Methods for Protecting Networks from Attacks

Networks are the backbone of modern information systems, connecting people, devices and applications. As such, network security is critical to protecting information and ensuring the confidentiality, integrity and availability of data. In this chapter, we will explore various methods for protecting networks from attacks.

C.1.   Firewalls

Firewalls are a critical component of network security, acting as a barrier between a trusted internal network and an untrusted external network, controlling incoming and outgoing data traffic. Firewalls can be used to block unauthorized access, monitor traffic and enforce security policies. Firewalls play a vital role in protecting against cyberattacks and unauthorized access, acts as the first line of defense against cyber threats, providing an added layer of security to the network. The purpose of a firewall is to prevent unauthorized access to the network while still allowing authorized users and applications to access the network.

Firewalls come in two main forms: hardware and software. Hardware firewalls are physical devices that are installed between the network and the internet, whereas software firewalls are installed on individual devices within the network. Both have their own unique features, benefits and drawbacks.

Hardware firewalls are physical devices that are installed on the network to protect against incoming and outgoing network traffic. They are designed to be placed between the Internet and the local network and they can be connected to the network through a wired or wireless connection. Hardware firewalls are often preferred by large organizations and enterprise networks due to their ability to handle high volumes of network traffic, which is critical in these environments. Software firewalls, on the other hand, are implemented as software programs that run on a computer or server within the network. They can be installed on individual computers or servers to provide protection for those specific devices. They are typically used in smaller networks or home networks because they are cheaper and relatively easy to install and maintain.

In terms of performance, hardware firewalls are generally considered to be faster and more reliable than software firewalls. This is because hardware firewalls are specifically designed for network security and are equipped with specialized hardware components that are optimized for this purpose. Hardware firewalls can handle large volumes of network traffic, making them ideal for large networks. Software firewalls are dependent on the performance of the computer or server on which they are installed. They can slow down the system and consume system resources, reducing the overall performance of the device. In some cases, this can make software firewalls unsuitable for high-performance network environments.

Hardware firewalls typically comes with an interface that provides access to the various features and functions, including the ability to create firewall rules, monitor network activity and perform regular updates. Software firewalls are managed through a software interface that is installed on the computer or server. The interface provides similar features and functions as hardware firewalls but it may not be as comprehensive as those found on hardware firewalls. In addition, software firewalls can be more complex to manage, particularly in larger networks where multiple firewalls may be deployed on multiple devices.

In terms of security, hardware firewalls are generally considered to be more secure than software ones. This is because hardware firewalls are specifically designed for network security and equipped with specialized hardware components. Software firewalls are more vulnerable to the same security threats compared to the hardware firewalls. They are more susceptible to malware, viruses and other security threats, which can compromise the security of the system or software firewall itself.

For example, if the network requires high performance and security, a hardware firewall may be the best option. On the other hand, if the network is smaller and doesn't require as much performance and security, a software firewall may be more suitable. It's also important to consider the budget and resources available for the firewall implementation, as hardware firewalls can be more expensive and require more technical expertise to manage than software firewalls.

In any case, it's important to use firewalls in combination with other security measures, such as antivirus software, intrusion detection and prevention systems and network access control, to ensure an effective security strategy.

Benefits of Firewalls

Protection against Cyber Threats: Firewalls provide an added layer of security against cyber threats, such as malware, viruses and hacking attempts, by controlling access to the network and filtering out malicious traffic.

Enhanced Privacy: Firewalls help protect sensitive data and prevent unauthorized access to confidential information. By controlling access to the network, firewalls can also prevent unauthorized access to personal information.

Improved Network Performance: Firewalls help prevent network congestion by filtering out unwanted traffic and controlling access to the network. This results in improved network performance and reduced downtime.

Compliance with Regulations: In many industries such as finance and healthcare, compliance with regulations is crucial. Firewalls help organizations comply with regulations by providing a secure and controlled environment for data transmission and storage.

C.2.   Intrusion Detection and Prevention Systems (IDS/IPS)

Intrusion Detection and Prevention Systems are network security devices that monitor network traffic and analyzing it for signs of suspicious or malicious activity. These systems are designed to detect and prevent unauthorized access to a computer network or system. When a potential attack is detected, the system can either alert security personnel or automatically block the traffic.

IDPS can be categorized into two types: network-based and host-based. Network-based IDPS monitor network traffic in real-time and analyze it for malicious activity. On the other hand Host-based IDPS are installed on individual computers or servers and monitor system activity for signs of intrusion.

IDPS can also be classified into two categories based on their functionality: intrusion detection systems (IDS) and intrusion prevention systems (IPS). IDS analyze network traffic for signs of intrusion while IPS not only detect but also prevent malicious activity from occurring.

The primary function of an IDPS is to identify and respond to security threats. These threats may include viruses, malware and other types of attacks. IDPS can detect these threats and alert the system administrator who can then take appropriate action to prevent the attack.

IDPS can also be used to monitor employee activity on the network. This can help prevent unauthorized access to sensitive data and prevent employees from engaging in activities that could compromise network security.

When selecting an IDPS, there are several factors to consider. These include the type of threats you are trying to prevent, size and complexity of your network and your budget. It's important to choose an IDPS that is easy to install, configure and maintain.

IDPS should also be updated regularly to keep up with the latest security threats. This includes installing security patches and updates as soon as they become available. Regular testing of the IDPS can also help identify any weaknesses or vulnerabilities in the system.

By selecting the right IDPS and keeping it updated, you can help protect your network from unauthorized access and keep your data secure.

C.3.   Virtual Private Networks (VPNs)

VPNs provide a secure, encrypted connection between two networks, allowing remote users to access internal resources as if they were directly connected to the network and can be used to protect data in transit and ensure the confidentiality of sensitive information. VPNs become increasingly popular in recent years as more people have become concerned about their online privacy and security.

VPN is a secure and private network connection that allows you to access the internet securely and anonymously. It works by encrypting your internet traffic and routing it through a remote server. This makes it difficult for anyone to monitor your online activity as your data is protected by encryption. Additionally, VPN can help you bypass geographic restrictions and censorship, allowing you to access content that may be blocked in your location. This can be particularly useful if you're traveling to a country where certain websites and services are unavailable.

One of the main benefits of using a VPN is enhanced online privacy. When you connect to a VPN, your internet service provider (ISP) is unable to monitor your online activity as all of your data is encrypted. This means that your browsing history, search queries and personal information are kept private.

Another benefit of using a VPN is increased security. When you connect to a public Wi-Fi network, your data is vulnerable to interception by hackers and other malicious actors. VPN encrypts your data, making it more difficult for hackers to intercept and steal your personal information.

When selecting a VPN, there are several factors to consider. These include the level of encryption, number of servers and locations and the speed of the connection. It's important to choose a VPN that offers strong encryption as well as a large number of servers and locations to ensure a fast and reliable connection.

It's also important to use a reputable VPN provider that takes your privacy seriously. Some free VPNs may collect and sell your data. So it's important to read reviews and choose a provider that has a good reputation for privacy and security.

By choosing the right VPN provider and following best practices for online security, you can ensure that your online activity remains private and secure.

C.4.   Network Access Control (NAC)

NAC is a security solution that helps organizations enforce security policies and control access to the network. NAC solutions typically involve checking the configuration of a device before allowing it to connect to the network and monitoring network traffic to ensure that only authorized devices and users are accessing the network.

NAC works by controlling access to the network based on several factors, including the user's identity, the device they are using and the security status of the device. Before a user is allowed to access the network, their device is checked to ensure that it meets the security requirements of the organization.

NAC can be implemented in several ways, including using software agents, network infrastructure devices or a combination of both. Software agents are installed on individual devices and are used to enforce security policies. Network infrastructure devices, such as switches and routers, can also be used to enforce security policies.

One of the main benefits of using NAC is increased security. By controlling access to the network organizations can prevent unauthorized users and devices from accessing their network resources. This can help prevent data breaches and other security incidents.

NAC can also be used to ensure compliance with security policies. For example, if an organization requires that all devices on their network have up to date antivirus software installed, NAC can be used to check that all devices meet this requirement before allowing them access to the network.

When selecting a NAC solution, there are several factors to consider. These include the level of security required, the number of devices that need to be supported and the complexity of the network. It's important to choose a solution that is easy to use and manage, as well as one that provides the necessary level of security for your organization.

NAC is an important component of network security. It helps organizations control access to their network resources and ensures compliance with security policies. By implementing NAC organizations can increase their security posture and prevent unauthorized access to their network.

C.5.   Encryption

We need to examine encryption with all details. Encryption is the process of converting data into an unreadable form to prevent unauthorized access. It can be used to protect data in transit and at rest, ensuring the confidentiality and integrity of sensitive information.

Encryption is a powerful technique that helps secure data from unauthorized access and ensures confidentiality, integrity and authenticity. In this chapter, we will delve into the world of encryption and explore how it can be used as a robust defense mechanism for safeguarding networks from attacks.

Understanding Encryption

Encryption is the process of converting plain text into unreadable and scrambled data, also known as ciphertext, using mathematical algorithms and cryptographic keys. The primary purpose of encryption is to prevent unauthorized access to sensitive information by making it indecipherable to anyone who does not possess the appropriate decryption key. Encryption is widely used to protect data in transit over networks, saved in storage devices and data in use during various computing processes.

There are two main types of encryption: symmetric and asymmetric. Symmetric encryption uses a single key for both encryption and decryption, meaning the same key is used to both lock and unlock the encrypted data. This type of encryption is relatively simple and efficient in terms of processing power but requires a secure method of key exchange between parties to ensure confidentiality. Examples of symmetric encryption algorithms include Advanced Encryption Standard (AES) and Data Encryption Standard (DES).

On the other hand, asymmetric encryption, also known as public-key encryption, uses a pair of keys: a public key and a private key. The public key is used for encryption, while the private key is used for decryption. The public key can be freely shared with anyonebut the private key must be kept secret by the owner. Asymmetric encryption provides a higher level of security as it eliminates the need for a secure key exchange process but it is generally slower and more computationally intensive compared to symmetric encryption. Examples of asymmetric encryption algorithms include RSA (Rivest-Shamir-Adleman), Diffie-Hellman, ECC (Elliptic Curve Cryptography), ECCSI (Elliptic Curve Cryptography-Based Signature with Identity), DSA (Digital Signature Algorithm), ElGamal, McEliece Cryptosystem, GPG (GNU Privacy Guard), S/MIME (Secure/Multipurpose Internet Mail Extensions), Blowfish, Camellia and Twofish.

RSA (Rivest-Shamir-Adleman): This is one of the most commonly used asymmetric encryption algorithms and it is named after its inventors Ron Rivest, Adi Shamir and Leonard Adleman. The algorithm was based on the mathematical concept of modular arithmetic and the difficulty of factoring large prime numbers into their factors. In its early years, RSA was primarily used for secure communication between the U.S. government and military. Since then, RSA has become one of the most widely used encryption algorithms in the world, used for everything from secure web browsing to online banking transactions. RSA has undergone several revisions and updates over the years to improve its security and performance but its underlying principles have remained the same.

RSA has many applications in online security. One of the most common uses is in secure web browsing using the HTTPS protocol. When you visit a website using HTTPS, your browser and the website's server negotiate a shared secret key using RSA encryption to encrypt all communication between the two parties.

RSA is also used for secure email communication using protocols like PGP (Pretty Good Privacy) and S/MIME (Secure/Multipurpose Internet Mail Extensions). These protocols use RSA to encrypt the email content and attachments to ensure that only the intended recipient can read the message.

In addition, RSA is used for secure file transfer using protocols like SSH (Secure Shell) and SFTP (Secure File Transfer Protocol). These protocols use RSA to authenticate the identity of the remote server and to encrypt the data being transferred.

Diffie-Hellman: This algorithm is used for secure key exchange over an unsecured communication channel. It allows two parties to generate a shared secret key without ever transmitting the key itself.

ECC (Elliptic Curve Cryptography): This algorithm is based on the mathematical properties of elliptic curves and is used for secure key exchange and digital signatures.

ECCSI (Elliptic Curve Cryptography-Based Signature with Identity): This is a digital signature algorithm that combines ECC and hash-based message authentication codes (HMACs) to provide secure digital signatures that are tied to a specific identity.

DSA (Digital Signature Algorithm): This algorithm is used for digital signatures and is based on the difficulty of computing discrete logarithms.

ElGamal: This is another encryption algorithm based on the difficulty of computing discrete logarithms. It is used for secure key exchange and digital signatures.

McEliece Cryptosystem: This is an asymmetric encryption algorithm that uses a different approach than most other algorithms. It is based on the difficulty of decoding a linear code and is considered to be one of the most secure encryption algorithms.

GPG (GNU Privacy Guard): This is a free implementation of the OpenPGP standard, which uses a combination of symmetric and asymmetric encryption for email and file encryption. GPG uses RSA for key exchange and digital signatures.

S/MIME (Secure/Multipurpose Internet Mail Extensions): This is a standard for secure email that uses both symmetric and asymmetric encryption. It uses RSA for key exchange and digital signatures.

Blowfish: This is a symmetric encryption algorithm but it is often used in combination with an asymmetric encryption algorithm like RSA for secure key exchange. Blowfish is known for its high speed and simplicity, making it a popular choice for encryption in software applications.

Camellia: This is a symmetric encryption algorithm that is based on the design of the AES algorithm. It is often used in combination with an asymmetric encryption algorithm like RSA for secure key exchange.

Twofish: This is a symmetric encryption algorithm that is known for its high security and flexibility. It is often used in combination with an asymmetric encryption algorithm like RSA for secure key exchange.

These are just a few examples of the many asymmetric encryption algorithms that are available. The choice of algorithm depends on factors like the level of security needed, the speed of the encryption and decryption process and the specific use case.

How Encryption Protects Networks from Attacks

Encryption serves as a powerful defense mechanism for protecting networks from attacks in several ways:

Confidentiality: Encryption ensures that data transmitted over networks or stored in storage devices remains confidential by rendering it unreadable to unauthorized parties. This prevents eavesdropping or interception of sensitive information by malicious actors attempting to gain unauthorized access to the network.

Integrity: Encryption helps maintain the integrity of data by protecting it from unauthorized modifications or tampering during transit or storage. Any alteration of the encrypted data results in an invalid decryption, alerting the intended recipient to the tampering attempt.

Authenticity: Encryption can be used to establish the authenticity of data by using digital signatures, which are created using private keys and can be verified using corresponding public keys. This helps verify the identity of the sender and ensures that the data has not been tampered with during transit.

Access Control: Encryption can be used as a form of access control by encrypting data stored on storage devices or transmitted over networks. This ensures that only authorized parties with the appropriate decryption keys can access the data, protecting against unauthorized access by cybercriminals or insider threats.

Defense against Man-in-the-Middle (MitM) Attacks: MitM attacks involve intercepting communications between two parties and gaining unauthorized access to the data being transmitted. Encryption can protect against MitM attacks by ensuring that the data being transmitted is encrypted and cannot be deciphered by the attacker.

Best Practices for Using Encryption to Protect Networks

To effectively use encryption as a method for protecting networks from attacks, the following best practices should be followed:

Use Strong Encryption Algorithms: Ensure that the encryption algorithms used are widely recognized and vetted by the security community for their strength and reliability. Avoid using weak or outdated encryption algorithms that may be susceptible to attacks.

Use Proper Key Management: Implement proper key management practices to ensure the secure generation, distribution, storage and revocation of encryption keys. Use separate keys for encryption and decryption and regularly rotate and update keys to minimize the risk of key compromise.

Implement End-to-End Encryption: Implement end-to-end encryption, where possible, to ensure that data is encrypted from the sender to the intended recipient. This prevents intermediaries, including service providers and network administrators, from accessing or tampering with the data.

Regularly Update and Patch Encryption Software: Keep encryption software up to date with the latest security patches and updates to protect against known vulnerabilities. Regularly review and update encryption configurations to align with industry best practices.

Use Multi-Factor Authentication: Implement multi-factor authentication for accessing encryption keys and systems to add an additional layer of security. This can help prevent unauthorized access even if encryption keys are compromised.

Train Employees on Encryption Best Practices: Educate employees about the importance of encryption and provide training on best practices for using encryption to protect sensitive data. This includes not sharing encryption keys, verifying the authenticity of encryption keys before use and understanding the proper use of encryption in different scenarios.

Regularly Monitor and Audit Encryption Implementation: Implement regular monitoring and auditing of encryption implementation to detect and respond to any potential vulnerabilities or anomalies. This includes reviewing logs, monitoring encryption processes and conducting regular security audits.

Encryption is a powerful method for protecting networks from attacks. It is a fundamental technology that is widely used to secure data in transit, data at rest and data in use. By implementing strong encryption algorithms, proper key management practices, end-to-end encryption, regular updates and patches, multi-factor authentication, employee training and monitoring and auditing, networks can be effectively safeguarded against attacks. Encryption should be an essential component of any comprehensive network security strategy, helping to ensure the confidentiality and integrity of sensitive data and protecting against unauthorized access.

II. WEB SECURITY

A. Overview

The World Wide Web has become an essential part of our daily lives, providing access to information, communication and commerce. As a result, the security of web-based systems has become increasingly important, as sensitive information and financial transactions are conducted online. In this chapter, we will provide an overview of web security and the challenges that organizations face when securing web-based systems.

Threats to Web Security

There are numerous threats to web security, including Cross-Site Scripting (XSS), Cross-Site Request Forgery (CSRF), SQL Injection, Remote Code Execution (RCE), Distributed Denial of Service (DDoS) attacks and Phishing attacks. These threats can lead to data theft, system compromise and loss of sensitive information.

Protecting Web Systems

There are several steps organizations can take to protect their web systems from attack, including:

Input Validation: Ensuring that data entered into web-based systems is validated to ensure that it meets certain requirements and is not malicious.

Encryption: Encrypting sensitive data, both in transit and at rest, to prevent unauthorized access.

Access Control: Implementing access controls to ensure that only authorized users can access sensitive information.

Security Awareness Training: Providing security awareness training for users to help prevent phishing attacks and other forms of social engineering.

Regular Security Updates: Keeping software and systems up to date with the latest security patches and updates.

Web security is an increasingly important aspect of information security, as more and more sensitive information and financial transactions are conducted online. By understanding the threats to web security and taking the necessary steps to protect web-based systems organizations can reduce the risk of data theft, system compromise and loss of sensitive information. In the next chapter, we will provide more in-depth information on specific web security technologies and techniques that organizations can use to protect their web systems.

B. Types of Web Attacks and How They Work

As the internet continues to grow and more people and organizations rely on it for communication, commerce and storage of sensitive information, the need for web security is becoming increasingly important. Web attacks are a common and growing threat and it is essential to understand the different types of attacks that exist and how they work in order to protect against them. In this chapter, we will examine several common types of web attacks and how they work.

B.1.   Cross-Site Scripting (XSS)

Cross-Site Scripting (XSS) is a type of web attack that involves injecting malicious code into a web page viewed by other users. The malicious code can be used to steal sensitive information, such as passwords and credit card numbers or to redirect the user to another website. XSS attacks can occur when a web application does not properly validate user input, allowing attackers to inject malicious code into the web page. XSS attacks are prevalent and can lead to the compromise of sensitive user data, theft of credentials and even full-scale system breaches. It's crucial to understand XSS thoroughly and learn how to defend against it effectively.

There are three main types of XSS attacks:

Reflected XSS: In this type of attack, the injected malicious script is included in a URL or form input and the server reflects that input back to the user without proper sanitization. When the user clicks on the URL or submits the form, the malicious script is executed in their browser.

Example:
Consider a web application that takes a search query as input and displays the results on the page. If the application does not properly sanitize the search query before displaying it, an attacker could inject a script in the search query, which would be reflected in the search results page. When other users click on the search result, the script is executed in their browsers, allowing the attacker to steal their data or perform other malicious actions.

Stored XSS: In this type of attack, the injected malicious script is permanently stored in a web application's database and is displayed to other users whenever the associated data is retrieved from the database and displayed on a web page.

Example:
Consider a comment section on a blog where users can leave comments. If the web application does not properly sanitize the comments before storing them in the database and displaying them on the blog post, an attacker could inject a script in their comment, which would be stored in the database. When other users view the blog post and the comments, the script is executed in their browsers, allowing the attacker to carry out malicious activities.

DOM-based XSS: In this type of attack, the malicious script is injected into the Document Object Model (DOM) of a web page and is executed directly in the victim's browser, without being sent to the server.

Example:
Consider a web application that uses JavaScript to dynamically update the content of a web page based on user input. If the application does not properly sanitize the user input before updating the DOM, an attacker could inject a script in the input, which would be executed in the victim's browser, allowing the attacker to manipulate the web page and steal data.

The Impact of XSS Attacks

XSS attacks can have severe consequences, including:

Data theft: XSS attacks can allow attackers to steal sensitive user data, such as usernames, passwords and credit card information.

Credential theft: XSS attacks can enable attackers to steal user credentials, allowing them to gain unauthorized access to user accounts and perform actions on behalf of the victim.

Web defacement: XSS attacks can be used to manipulate the content of web pages, defacing them with malicious or inappropriate content, which can damage the reputation of the affected website or organization.

Malware delivery: XSS attacks can be used to deliver malware to unsuspecting users, infecting their systems and causing further damage.

Case Study: "XSS Worm" Attack

One notorious example of an XSS attack is the "Samy" worm that hit the social networking website Myspace back in 2005. The worm exploited a stored XSS vulnerability in Myspace's profile page to inject a malicious script into the profiles of affected users. When other users viewed these profiles, the script was executed in their browsers, adding the worm to their profiles as well. Within a matter of hours, the worm had spread to millions of profiles, causing widespread disruption and damage.

The Samy worm not only defaced the profiles with a message but also added the attacker as a friend, causing an exponential spread of the worm. It resulted in MySpace having to shut down the site temporarily to contain the spread and fix the vulnerability. This incident highlights the destructive potential of XSS attacks and the need for robust security measures to protect against them.

Mitigation Techniques for XSS Attacks

Input Validation and Sanitization: Always validate and sanitize any user input, including URL parameters, form data and data stored in databases, before including them in web pages. Use secure coding practices and libraries that provide built-in functions for encoding user input to prevent XSS attacks.

Example:
Instead of directly inserting user input into an HTML element, use functions such as htmlspecialchars() or htmlentities() in PHP or equivalent encoding functions in other programming languages to encode special characters and prevent script execution.

Content Security Policy (CSP): Implement CSP, a security feature that allows you to specify which sources of content are allowed to be loaded by a web page, thereby mitigating XSS attacks. CSP provides an additional layer of defense by blocking the execution of scripts from unauthorized sources.

Example:

Set the Content-Security-Policy header in your web server configuration or meta tag in your HTML to specify allowed sources for scripts, images, styles and other resources.

Secure HTTP-Only Cookies: Use HTTP-only cookies to store sensitive data, such as session tokens or user credentials. HTTP-only cookies cannot be accessed by JavaScript, which helps prevent XSS attacks from stealing sensitive data from cookies.

Example:

Set the HttpOnly flag when setting cookies in your web application to prevent client-side scripts from accessing the cookies.

Regular Security Patching: Stay up to date with the latest security patches and updates for your web application framework, libraries and server software. XSS vulnerabilities can be patched through updates and it's essential to promptly apply these patches to protect against known vulnerabilities.

User Education and Awareness: Educate your users about the risks of XSS attacks and encourage them to be cautious with their interactions on websites, especially when clicking on links or entering personal information. Promote safe browsing habits and report any suspicious activities or unexpected behaviors on websites.

Cross-Site Scripting (XSS) is a serious web vulnerability that can have severe consequences if not properly addressed. As an online security expert, it's crucial to understand the different types of XSS attacks, their impact and effective mitigation techniques. By implementing input validation and sanitization, using Content Security Policy (CSP), using secure HTTP-only cookies, regularly patching security vulnerabilities and educating users, you can significantly reduce the risk of XSS attacks and protect your web applications and users from potential harm.

Remember, staying vigilant, keeping up to date with the latest security best practices and regularly testing your web applications for vulnerabilities are essential in maintaining a secure online environment. Stay proactive, be thorough in your defense against XSS attacks and safeguard the confidentiality, integrity and availability of your web applications and user data.

B.2.   SQL Injection

SQL Injection is a type of web attack that involves injecting malicious code into a website's database. The attack allows the attacker to access, modify or delete sensitive information stored in the database. SQL Injection attacks can occur when a web application does not properly validate user input, allowing attackers to inject malicious code into the database. This type of attack can have devastating consequences, including unauthorized data access, data modification and even data deletion. In this chapter, we will delve into the details of SQL Injection, its various forms and how you can protect your database against it.

At its core, SQL Injection occurs when an attacker is able to inject malicious SQL code into a web application's query parameters, which are then executed against the database. This allows the attacker to manipulate the SQL query in unintended ways, bypassing authentication and authorization checks and gaining access to sensitive data or making unauthorized modifications to the database.

There are several common ways through which SQL Injection attacks can be carried out. Let's take a look at some of the most common types of SQL Injection attacks:

Union-Based SQL Injection: In this type of attack, an attacker appends a UNION statement to the original query, allowing them to combine the results of multiple SELECT statements into a single result set. By doing so, the attacker can retrieve data from other tables in the database that they are not authorized to access.

Error-Based SQL Injection: In this type of attack, an attacker exploits error messages generated by the database to gain information about the structure of the database and retrieve sensitive data. For example, if an attacker enters a SQL query that generates an error, the error message returned by the database may contain valuable information such as table names, column names and even actual data.

Blind SQL Injection: This type of attack is more subtle and harder to detect, as it does not generate any error messages. Instead, the attacker crafts SQL queries that return boolean (true/false) responses or no responses at all and then uses the application's behavior to infer information about the database. This can include guessing the length of a password or extracting data one character at a time.

Protecting Against SQL Injection Attacks

Use Prepared Statements or Parameterized Queries: Prepared statements or parameterized queries are a powerful defense against SQL Injection attacks. They allow you to separate SQL code from user input, ensuring that user-supplied data is treated as data and not as part of the SQL query. Prepared statements use placeholders for user input, which are then bound to actual values, eliminating the need for string concatenation and making it virtually impossible for an attacker to inject malicious SQL code.

Sanitize User Input: Always validate and sanitize any user input that is used in constructing SQL queries. This includes data from user input fields, query parameters and any other external sources. Sanitizing user input involves removing or escaping any characters that may have special meaning in SQL queries, such as single quotes, double quotes and backslashes. Be cautious when using user input directly in SQL queries and avoid using user input as part of SQL query construction without proper sanitization.

Limit Database User Permissions: Restrict the permissions of the database user used by the web application to the bare minimum necessary for its operation. Avoid using privileged users, such as the database administrator, for normal application operations. Instead, create separate database users with limited permissions that only have access to the specific tables and operations required by the application. This limits the potential damage that can be caused by a SQL Injection attack, as the attacker's access will be restricted to the permissions of the compromised user.

Implement Least Privilege Principle: Follow the principle of least privilege, which means that users and applications should only have the minimum necessary permissions to perform their tasks. Avoid using overly permissive permissions, such as granting 'ALL PRIVILEGES' to database users or using overly broad query permissions. Regularly review and update the permissions of your database users to ensure that they are only granted the permissions they need and nothing more.

Keep Software and Libraries Up to date: SQL Injection attacks can often exploit known vulnerabilities in software and libraries used by web applications. It's crucial to keep all software, including the database management system, web server and any libraries or frameworks, up to date with the latest security patches and updates. Regularly monitor for security advisories and patches released by software vendors and apply them promptly to protect against known vulnerabilities.

Use Web Application Firewalls (WAFs): Web Application Firewalls (WAFs) can provide an additional layer of protection against SQL Injection attacks. WAFs can intercept and analyze incoming HTTP requests and responses, filtering out malicious SQL code or other suspicious patterns of behavior. Many WAFs also have built-in SQL Injection protection rulesets that can detect and block known SQL Injection attacks. However, it's important to note that WAFs are not a substitute for proper coding practices and secure database configurations and should be used in conjunction with other security measures.

Implement Input Validation: Implement strict input validation on user-supplied data to ensure that only expected characters and data types are allowed. For example, if a field is expected to contain an integer, validate that the input is indeed an integer before using it in a SQL query. This can help prevent SQL Injection attacks that rely on injecting unexpected data types or characters into the query.

Regular Security Audits: Conduct regular security audits of your web application and database to identify and fix potential vulnerabilities, including SQL Injection vulnerabilities. This can include code reviews, vulnerability scanning and penetration testing. Regularly review and analyze application logs and database logs to detect any suspicious activity that may indicate a SQL Injection attack.

Educate and Train Your Development Team: Properly educate and train your development team on secure coding practices, including how to write SQL queries safely, validate and sanitize user input and follow other best practices for protecting against SQL Injection attacks. Provide regular training sessions and resources to keep your development team up to date with the latest security techniques and technologies.

SQL Injection attacks continue to be a persistent threat to web applications and databases. However, by following best practices such as using prepared statements or parameterized queries, sanitizing user input, limiting database user permissions, implementing the least privilege principle, keeping software and libraries up to date, using web application firewalls, implementing input validation, conducting regular security audits and educating and training your development team, you can significantly reduce the risk of SQL Injection attacks.

In addition to the technical measures discussed in this chapter, it's also important to foster a security-conscious culture within your organization. Encourage a proactive approach to security among your development team and promote a culture of continuous learning and improvement. Emphasize the importance of security awareness and the role that each team member plays in protecting the web application and its data from SQL Injection attacks and other security threats.

Finally, in the event of a suspected or confirmed SQL Injection attack, it's crucial to have an incident response plan in place. This plan should outline the steps to take in case of a security breach, including isolating the affected systems, mitigating the damage, notifying relevant stakeholders and conducting a thorough investigation to identify the root cause and prevent future attacks.

B.3.   Man-in-the-Middle (MitM)

Man-in-the-Middle (MitM) attacks are a type of web attack that involves intercepting communication between a user and a website. The attacker intercepts the communication, eavesdrops on the conversation and can even modify the data being transmitted. MitM attacks can occur when a user connects to an unsecured Wi-Fi network or when an attacker is able to intercept communication between a user and a website. In this chapter, we will explore the types, techniques and countermeasures for MitM attacks and discuss the best practices for mitigating and preventing them.

Types of MitM Attacks:

There are several types of MitM attacks, each with its own method of interception and exploitation. These include:

IP Spoofing: An attacker manipulates the source address of a packet to make it appear as if it originated from a trusted source. This allows the attacker to intercept, modify and inject packets into a network, making it difficult to trace the origin of the attack.

DNS Spoofing: An attacker manipulates DNS (Domain Name System) queries and responses to redirect traffic to a fake website or server. This can be used to steal sensitive information, such as login credentials and credit card details.

HTTPS Spoofing: An attacker uses a fake SSL/TLS certificate to impersonate a legitimate website and intercept communication between the user and the server. This allows the attacker to view and modify sensitive data, such as passwords, personal information and financial transactions.

Session Hijacking: An attacker steals the session cookie of a user to gain unauthorized access to a website or web application. This can be achieved through various methods, such as sniffing network traffic, stealing cookies stored on the victim's device and exploiting vulnerabilities in the website or web application.

Techniques for MitM Attacks:

MitM attacks can be carried out using various techniques, some of which include:

Packet Sniffing: An attacker intercepts and analyses packets of data transmitted over a network to extract sensitive information, such as login credentials, credit card details and personal information.

ARP Spoofing: An attacker intercepts ARP (Address Resolution Protocol) messages to map the MAC (Media Access

Control) address of a network device to its IP address. This allows the attacker to redirect traffic to a fake website or server.

Session Replay: An attacker intercepts and replays session data to gain unauthorized access to a website or web application. This can be achieved through various methods, such as intercepting cookies, intercepting HTTP requests and responses and intercepting SSL/TLS handshakes.

SSL Stripping: An attacker downgrades an HTTPS connection to an HTTP connection, allowing the attacker to intercept and modify the communication between the user and the server.

Countermeasures for MitM Attacks:

There are various countermeasures that can be used to mitigate and prevent MitM attacks. These include:

Using HTTPS: Websites and web applications should use HTTPS (HTTP Secure) to encrypt communication between the user and the server. This helps to prevent SSL/TLS spoofing and session hijacking attacks.

Using SSL Pinning: SSL pinning involves hardcoding the SSL/TLS certificate of a website or web application into the client's software, making it difficult for an attacker to use a fake SSL/TLS certificate to impersonate the website or web application.

Using DNSSEC: DNSSEC (Domain Name System Security Extensions) adds a layer of security to DNS by verifying the authenticity of DNS queries and responses, making it more difficult for an attacker to carry out DNS spoofing attacks.

Using VPN: A VPN (Virtual Private Network) encrypts network traffic and routes it through a secure tunnel, making it more difficult for an attacker to intercept and eavesdrop on communication.

Regularly updating software and devices: Regularly updating software and devices can help to patch vulnerabilities that could be exploited by MitM attackers. This includes updating operating systems, web browsers, antivirus software and firmware.

Two-Factor Authentication: Two-factor authentication adds an extra layer of security to login credentials by requiring a second form of authentication, such as a one-time password or biometric authentication. This makes it more difficult for an attacker to hijack a user's session and gain unauthorized access.

Best Practices for Mitigating and Preventing MitM Attacks:

To effectively mitigate and prevent MitM attacks, it is important to follow some best practices, including:

Always use HTTPS: Websites and web applications should use HTTPS to encrypt communication between the user and the server.

Avoid Public Wi-Fi: Public Wi-Fi hotspots are often unsecured, making them a prime target for MitM attackers. Avoid using public Wi-Fi hotspots or use a VPN to encrypt your network traffic.

Keep Software and Devices Updated: Regularly update software and devices to patch vulnerabilities that could be exploited by MitM attackers.

Use Two-Factor Authentication: Two-factor authentication adds an extra layer of security to login credentials, making it more difficult for an attacker to hijack a user's session and gain unauthorized access.

Be Vigilant: Be vigilant when browsing the internet and avoid clicking on suspicious links or downloading unknown software.

MitM attacks are a serious threat to online security and can have devastating consequences, including identity theft, financial loss and reputational damage. By understanding the types, techniques and countermeasures for MitM attacks and following best practices for mitigating and preventing them, individuals and organizations can better protect themselves from these types of cyberattacks. It is important to remain vigilant and proactive in the fight against MitM attacks and to stay up to date with the latest security measures and best practices.

B.4. Distributed Denial of Service (DDoS)

Distributed Denial of Service (DDoS) attacks are a type of web attack that involves overwhelming a website with traffic from multiple sources, causing the website to become unavailable to users. DDoS attacks can be launched using a network of compromised computers known as a botnet or using other methods to generate large amounts of traffic.

These are just a few examples of the many types of web attacks that exist. Understanding how these attacks work and the methods used by attackers is crucial for organizations looking to protect their web applications and sensitive information.

As more and more businesses and individuals rely on the internet for communication, transactions and data storage, the threat of Distributed Denial of Service (DDoS) attacks looms large. In this chapter, we will examine the world of DDoS attacks, understanding their nature, impact and most importantly, how to effectively protect against them.

What is a DDoS Attack?

A DDoS attack is a malicious attempt to disrupt the availability of a website, server or online service by overwhelming it with traffic from multiple sources. In a typical DDoS attack, a large number of compromised devices, known as "botnets," are used to send an excessive amount of requests to the target system, causing it to become unresponsive or crash. These botnets are often created using malware that infects vulnerable devices such as computers, servers, routers and Internet of Things (IoT) devices and enlists them into a network of bots under the control of the attacker.

DDoS attacks can have severe consequences for businesses and individuals, resulting in financial losses, reputational damage and disruption of operations. Therefore, it is crucial to understand the different types of DDoS attacks and their potential impacts in order to effectively protect against them.

Types of DDoS Attacks

DDoS attacks can take various forms, each with its own unique characteristics. Some of the most common types of DDoS attacks include:

Volumetric Attacks: These attacks aim to overwhelm the target system with a massive volume of traffic, consuming its bandwidth and resources. Volumetric attacks are typically carried out using botnets that generate a huge number of requests, such as UDP floods, ICMP floods and DNS amplification attacks.

Protocol Attacks: These attacks exploit vulnerabilities in the network protocols or applications of the target system, causing it to become unresponsive or crash. Examples of protocol attacks include SYN floods, ACK floods and Smurf attacks.

Application Layer Attacks: These attacks target the application layer of the target system, aiming to exhaust its resources or exploit vulnerabilities in the web applications. Common application layer attacks include HTTP floods, Slowloris attacks and SQL injection attacks.

Reflective/Amplified Attacks: These attacks exploit the vulnerabilities of certain protocols, such as DNS or NTP, to generate a large amount of traffic that is reflected or amplified towards the target system, overwhelming its resources. This type of attack can result in massive traffic volumes, making it extremely difficult to mitigate.

Impacts of DDoS Attacks

DDoS attacks can have significant impacts on businesses, individuals and the overall online ecosystem. Some of the potential consequences of DDoS attacks include:

Financial Losses: Downtime caused by DDoS attacks can result in lost revenue, especially for businesses that rely heavily on their online presence for sales, customer engagement or service delivery. The cost of mitigating and recovering from a DDoS attack, including investing in additional infrastructure and security measures, can also be substantial.

Reputational Damage: A successful DDoS attack can tarnish a business's reputation, leading to loss of customer trust and loyalty. Customers may perceive a business as unreliable or insecure if its online services are frequently unavailable due to DDoS attacks.

Operational Disruption: DDoS attacks can disrupt normal business operations, causing delays, disruptions and additional workload for IT and security teams. This can lead to loss of productivity, missed deadlines and increased operational costs.

Legal and Regulatory Consequences: Depending on the nature of the business and the data being handled, DDoS attacks can have legal and regulatory implications. For example, if a DDoS attack results in a data breach or loss of confidential information, the business may face legal action, fines or other penalties.

Protecting Against DDoS Attacks

Given the severe consequences of DDoS attacks, it is crucial for businesses and individuals to take proactive measures to protect against them. Some of the best practices for protecting against DDoS attacks include:

Use of Anti-DDoS Solutions: One of the most effective ways to protect against DDoS attacks is to use anti-DDoS solutions. These solutions use various techniques, such as traffic filtering, rate limiting and behavioral analysis, to detect and mitigate DDoS attacks in real-time. Many hosting providers and cloud services offer anti-DDoS solutions as part of their service offerings.

Regular Security Audits: Conducting regular security audits of network infrastructure, applications and devices can help identify and remediate vulnerabilities that can be exploited by DDoS attacks. This includes patching and updating software, disabling unnecessary services and configuring firewalls and intrusion detection/prevention systems.

Implementing Access Controls: Implementing access controls, such as firewalls, VPNs and two-factor authentication, can help prevent unauthorized access to network resources and devices. This can limit the potential for DDoS attacks and other types of cyber threats.

Educating Employees: Educating employees on best practices for online security, such as avoiding suspicious links and emails, using strong passwords and reporting suspicious activity, can help reduce the risk of DDoS attacks and other types of cyber threats.

DDoS attacks pose a significant threat to businesses, individuals and the overall online ecosystem. By implementing best practices, such as using anti-DDoS solutions, conducting regular security audits, implementing access controls and educating employees, businesses and individuals can reduce the risk of DDoS attacks and ensure a safer and more secure online environment.

C. Methods for Protecting Websites and Web Applications From Attacks

With the growing number of network attacks and security threats, it is important to take proactive measures to protect networks and systems. In this chapter, we will provide an overview of the methods that can be used to protect networks from attacks.

C.1.   Firewalls

As we examined before, firewalls are a key tool in network security. A firewall is a network security device that monitors and controls incoming and outgoing network traffic based on predetermined security rules. They act as a barrier between internal networks and the internet, filtering incoming and outgoing traffic based on predefined rules. Firewalls can be hardware-based or software-based and can provide protection against a wide range of attacks. In this chapter, we will discuss the various types of firewalls, their functions and best practices for implementing and managing them.

Types of Firewalls

There are several types of firewalls, each with their own unique strengths and weaknesses. Some of the most common types of firewalls include:

Packet Filtering Firewalls: Packet filtering firewalls are the most basic type of firewall. They work by examining each packet of data that passes through the network and comparing it against a set of predefined rules. Packets that meet the criteria of the rules are allowed to pass, while those that do not are blocked. While packet filtering firewalls are relatively easy to configure and manage, they provide limited security since they only examine the packet header and not the packet content.

Stateful Inspection Firewalls: Stateful inspection firewalls, also known as dynamic packet filtering firewalls, examine the complete packet contents and keep track of the connection state. They can determine if a packet belongs to an established connection or if it is an unauthorized connection attempt. While stateful inspection firewalls provide a higher level of security than packet filtering firewalls, they are more complex to configure and can have a higher resource overhead.

Application-Level Firewalls: Application-level firewalls, also known as proxy firewalls, operate at the application layer of the network stack. They act as an intermediary between the client and the server and inspect the entire application payload. This allows them to provide more granular control over network traffic and block specific types of traffic, such as malware or malicious requests. However, they can have a higher latency and can be more difficult to manage than other types of firewalls.

Next Generation Firewalls: Next generation firewalls are a more advanced type of firewall that incorporates additional security features such as intrusion prevention, malware detection and content filtering. They use advanced algorithms to analyze network traffic and identify potential threats. They also provide more detailed reporting and logging capabilities. Next-generation firewalls are often used in high-security environments, such as government agencies and financial institutions.

Functions of Firewalls

Firewalls serve several critical functions in network security. Some of the most important functions of firewalls include:

Traffic Filtering: Firewalls filter network traffic based on predetermined rules. This allows them to block unwanted traffic, such as malicious packets or unauthorized access attempts.

Access Control: Firewalls control access to network resources by allowing or denying traffic based on predefined rules. This ensures that only authorized users can access sensitive data and resources.

Network Address Translation (NAT): Firewalls can perform NAT, which allows multiple devices on a network to share a single IP address. This can help protect against attacks by hiding the internal IP addresses from external networks.

VPN and Remote Access: Firewalls can provide VPN and remote access capabilities. This allows remote users to securely connect to the network and access network resources.

Best Practices for Implementing and Managing Firewalls

To ensure the maximum effectiveness of firewalls, it is essential to implement and manage them correctly. Some best practices for implementing and managing firewalls include:

Define and Enforce Firewall Policies: It is crucial to define and enforce firewall policies that align with business goals and security requirements. Firewall policies should be regularly reviewed and updated to ensure they remain relevant and effective.

Implement a Multi-Layered Defense Strategy: Firewalls should be part of a multi-layered defense strategy that includes other security measures such as intrusion prevention, anti-virus and anti-malware solutions. This provides additional layers of protection and reduces the risk of a successful attack.

Regularly Update and Patch Firewalls: Firewalls, like any software, can have vulnerabilities that can be exploited by attackers. To prevent this, it is essential to keep firewalls up to date with the latest patches and updates. This helps ensure that any known vulnerabilities are patched and that the firewall remains secure.

Configure Firewalls with Least Privilege: Firewalls should be configured with the principle of least privilege in mind. This means that only the minimum necessary access should be granted to users and applications. By limiting access to network resources, the risk of unauthorized access and data breaches is reduced.

Monitor Firewall Activity: Firewalls should be regularly monitored for suspicious activity. This can be done through event logs, alerts and other monitoring tools. Monitoring firewall activity helps identify potential security breaches and enables quick action to be taken to mitigate any risks.

Regularly Test Firewall Security: Regularly testing firewall security is essential to identify any weaknesses or vulnerabilities. Penetration testing and vulnerability assessments can help identify potential vulnerabilities that could be exploited by attackers. By testing firewall security, potential weaknesses can be identified and addressed before they can be exploited.

Firewalls play a critical role in online security by protecting networks from unauthorized access and cyber attacks. By implementing and managing firewalls correctly organizations can significantly reduce the risk of data breaches and cyber attacks. As technology evolves, it is essential to keep firewalls up to date and to continuously evaluate and adjust firewall policies and configurations to ensure maximum effectiveness.

C.2.   Encryption

Encryption is a method of converting plaintext into ciphertext, making it unreadable to unauthorized parties. Encryption can be used to protect sensitive information, such as passwords, financial information and personal information, from being intercepted and read by unauthorized parties.

We examined encryption before at "Methods for Protecting Networks from Attacks" chapter.

C.3.   Intrusion Detection and Prevention Systems (IDPS)

Intrusion Detection and Prevention Systems (IDPS) are an important part of any comprehensive cybersecurity strategy. Those systems monitor network traffic for signs of attack or intrusion. IDPS can be configured to detect specific types of attacks and can also be set up to automatically block incoming traffic that matches certain criteria.

IDPS help organizations identify and respond to potential security incidents in real-time. This chapter will explore the key concepts of IDPS, types of IDPS and best practices for implementing and maintaining an effective IDPS.

What is an Intrusion Detection and Prevention System?

IDPS is a software or hardware system that monitors network and system activities for malicious behavior or policy violations. IDPS are designed to detect, alert and respond to potential security incidents in real-time. IDPS can help organizations prevent unauthorized access, data theft and other cyber attacks by detecting and stopping potential threats before they cause damage.

Types of IDPS

There are several types of IDPS, each with its unique strengths and weaknesses. The following are the three primary types of IDPS:

Network-based IDPS: Network-based IDPS monitor network traffic for signs of malicious activity. Network-based IDPS can detect threats such as port scanning, denial-of-service attacks and malware propagation. Network-based IDPS are deployed at key points within the network infrastructure, such as routers, switches and firewalls.

Host-based IDPS: Host-based IDPS monitor activity on individual hosts, such as servers and workstations. Host-based IDPS can detect threats such as malware infections, unauthorized access and data exfiltration. Host-based IDPS are typically installed on each host and monitor local system activity.

Hybrid IDPS: Hybrid IDPS combine the capabilities of network-based and host-based IDPS. Hybrid IDPS can monitor network traffic and host activity, providing a more comprehensive view of potential threats. Hybrid IDPS are deployed at key points within the network infrastructure and on individual hosts.

Best Practices for Implementing and Maintaining an Effective IDPS

Implementing and maintaining an effective IDPS requires careful planning and execution. The following are some best practices for implementing and maintaining an effective IDPS:

Define Security Policies: Define security policies that govern the behavior of IDPS. Security policies should outline the types of activities that are allowed and those that are prohibited. Security policies should also define the threshold for triggering alerts and notifications.

Choose the Right Type of IDPS: Choose the type of IDPS that is best suited for your organization's needs. Network-based IDPS are ideal for large organizations with complex network infrastructures, while host-based IDPS are ideal for small to medium-sized organizations with a limited number of hosts. Hybrid IDPS provide the most comprehensive view of potential threats but require a higher level of resources.

Configure IDPS Properly: Configure IDPS according to your organization's security policies. This includes setting up alert thresholds, defining exclusion rules and configuring response actions.

Regularly Update IDPS: Regularly update IDPS to ensure that it has the latest security patches and threat intelligence. Regular updates help to keep IDPS effective in detecting and responding to potential threats.

Monitor IDPS Activity: Monitor IDPS activity to ensure that it is functioning properly and detecting potential threats. Regular monitoring can help identify issues or gaps in the security posture of the organization.

Conduct Regular Testing: Conduct regular testing of IDPS to ensure that it is effective in detecting and responding to potential threats. Penetration testing and vulnerability scanning can help identify weaknesses in the IDPS and inform improvements.

Train Personnel: Train personnel on the proper use and maintenance of IDPS. Personnel should understand how to respond to alerts and notifications and how to report potential security incidents.

Intrusion Detection and Prevention Systems are critical components of any organization's cybersecurity strategy. They help detect and respond to potential security incidents in real-time, preventing unauthorized access, data theft and other cyber attacks. In this chapter, we explored the key concepts of IDPS, types of IDPS including network-based, host-based and hybrid IDPS, as well as best practices for implementing and maintaining an effective IDPS.

Implementing and maintaining an effective IDPS requires careful planning, proper configuration, regular updates, monitoring, testing and personnel training. By defining security policies, choosing the right type of IDPS, configuring it properly, regularly updating it, monitoring its activity, conducting regular testing and training personnel organizations can enhance their cybersecurity posture and effectively protect their websites and web applications from attacks.

It's important to remember that IDPS are not a one-size-fits-all solution and should be tailored to the specific needs and resources of each organization. Regular reviews and updates of IDPS policies, configurations and technologies are necessary to adapt to the evolving threat landscape and ensure optimal performance.

It's essential for organizations to invest in IDPS as part of their overall cybersecurity strategy and stay vigilant in keeping their IDPS up to date and effective in the ever-evolving landscape of cyber threats. With the right IDPS in place and proper management organizations can significantly enhance their online security posture and protect their digital assets.

C.4.   Virtual Private Networks (VPNs):

VPNs can be used to protect sensitive information and to ensure that remote users are able to access internal networks securely. They are becoming increasingly popular in today's digital age as more organizations and individuals seek to protect their online activities from prying eyes. In this chapter, we will discuss the key concepts of VPNs, how they work, the different types of VPNs and their role in protecting websites and web applications from attacks.

What is a VPN?

A VPN is a secure, encrypted connection between a client device and a remote server over the internet. It creates a private network within the public internet by encrypting all traffic between the client device and the remote server. This ensures that any data transmitted between the two endpoints is secure and private.

How do VPNs work?

When a client device connects to a VPN, it creates an encrypted tunnel between the device and the VPN server. All data transmitted between the two endpoints is encrypted and can only be decrypted by the client and the VPN server. This means that any third-party intercepting the data will only see gibberish and not be able to access the actual data.

The VPN server acts as an intermediary between the client device and the internet. All requests from the client device are sent to the VPN server, which then sends them on to the internet. The VPN server then receives the response from the internet and sends it back to the client device through the encrypted tunnel.

Types of VPNs

There are two main types of VPNs: remote access VPNs and site-to-site VPNs.

Remote access VPNs are typically used by individual users to securely connect to a corporate network from a remote location. They provide a secure, encrypted connection to the corporate network, allowing remote workers to access resources on the network as if they were physically present in the office.

Site-to-site VPNs, on the other hand, are used to connect two or more networks together securely over the internet. They create a virtual network between the different sites, allowing traffic to be securely transmitted between them.

Benefits of VPNs

VPNs offer several benefits when it comes to protecting websites and web applications from attacks. Firstly, they encrypt all traffic between the client device and the remote server, making it impossible for attackers to intercept and read the data. This is particularly important when transmitting sensitive information such as login credentials, financial data and personal information.

Secondly, VPNs can help protect against Man-in-the-Middle (MitM) attacks. In a MitM attack, an attacker intercepts communication between two parties and masquerades as one of the parties to gain access to sensitive information. With a VPN, all data is encrypted and transmitted securely, making it much harder for attackers to intercept and tamper with the data.

Finally, VPNs can help protect against Distributed Denial of Service (DDoS) attacks. In a DDoS attack, an attacker floods a website or web application with traffic, overwhelming the server and causing it to crash. By routing traffic through a VPN, the VPN server can act as a buffer between the client device and the internet, preventing the server from being overwhelmed by traffic.

Implementing and Maintaining an Effective VPN

To implement an effective VPN organizations must choose the right type of VPN for their needs and resources, properly configure it, regularly update it and train personnel on its use. It's important to choose a VPN provider that is trustworthy and has a good reputation for security.

Organizations should also ensure that their VPN is properly configured with strong encryption and authentication protocols. Regular updates to the VPN software should be applied to address any vulnerabilities or bugs that may be discovered.

Finally, personnel training is critical to ensure that VPNs are used properly and securely. Employees should be trained on the proper use of VPNs, including how to connect and disconnect from the VPN, how to identify potential security risks and how to report any issues or concerns. It's also important to educate employees about the importance of not sharing VPN credentials, using strong and unique passwords and being cautious when accessing websites and web applications while connected to the VPN.

Challenges and Considerations

While VPNs are a powerful tool for protecting websites and web applications from attacks, there are also challenges and considerations to keep in mind. Some of these challenges include:

Performance impact: Encrypting and decrypting data can add overhead to the network, which may result in reduced performance. Organizations need to carefully evaluate the impact of VPNs on network performance and consider factors such as bandwidth, latency and scalability.

Trustworthiness of VPN providers: Not all VPN providers are created equal and it's important to choose a reputable and trustworthy VPN provider. Some VPN providers may log user data, which may compromise the privacy and security of the VPN connection. Organizations should thoroughly research and evaluate VPN providers before selecting one for their needs.

Potential for VPN leaks: VPN leaks occur when the VPN connection fails to encrypt all traffic, allowing some data to leak outside of the encrypted tunnel. This can happen due to misconfigurations, software vulnerabilities or other issues. Organizations should regularly test for VPN leaks and take steps to address any vulnerabilities that may be identified.

Compliance and legal considerations: Organizations must also consider compliance and legal requirements when implementing VPNs. Depending on the industry and location, there may be regulations and laws that govern the use of VPNs, such as data privacy laws, data localization requirements and export control regulations. Organizations should ensure that their use of VPNs aligns with these requirements.

User awareness and training: Educating employees about the proper use of VPNs and the risks associated with improper use is crucial. Users need to be aware of the importance of protecting their VPN credentials, avoiding risky online behaviors while connected to the VPN and promptly reporting any issues or concerns. Regular training and awareness programs can help ensure that employees are vigilant and responsible when using VPNs.

Virtual Private Networks (VPNs) are a valuable tool for protecting websites and web applications from attacks. They provide a secure, encrypted connection between client devices and remote servers, ensuring that data transmitted over the internet is secure and private. By encrypting data and routing traffic through a VPN organizations can protect against interception, tampering and DDoS attacks. However, implementing and maintaining an effective VPN requires careful consideration of performance impact, trustworthiness of VPN providers, potential for leaks, compliance and legal requirements and user awareness and training.

In summary, VPNs are a powerful tool in the online security arsenal and can provide an additional layer of protection for websites and web applications. By carefully selecting a trustworthy VPN provider, configuring the VPN properly, keeping it up to date and educating users on its proper use organizations can enhance their security posture and mitigate the risk of attacks.

C.5. Access Control

Access control is a fundamental component of online security. It involves the process of determining who can access specific resources, data or functionality within a website or web application. Access control mechanisms are used to ensure that only authorized users can access sensitive data or functionality, while unauthorized users are denied access. In this chapter, we will discuss access control and its role in protecting websites and web applications from attacks.

Types of Access Control

There are several types of access control mechanisms that can be used to protect websites and web applications. These include:

Role-based Access Control (RBAC): RBAC is a popular access control model that grants permissions to users based on their roles within an organization. Users are assigned to specific roles and those roles are granted access to specific resources or functionality. This model is easy to manage and can be used to enforce security policies across an organization.

Attribute-based Access Control (ABAC): ABAC is a more flexible access control model that grants permissions based on a combination of attributes, such as the user's role, location, time of day and other factors. This model allows for more granular control over access to resources but can be more complex to manage.

Discretionary Access Control (DAC): DAC is a model where the owner of a resource or file determines who can access it. This model is less secure than RBAC or ABAC because it relies on the discretion of the owner to determine access rights.

Mandatory Access Control (MAC): MAC is a model where access rights are determined by a central authority. This model is often used in high-security environments, such as government or military organizations, where access to sensitive data or resources is strictly controlled.

Access Control Best Practices

To ensure effective access control and protect websites and web applications from attacks, there are several best practices that organizations should follow:

Principle of Least Privilege: This principle states that users should be granted the minimum level of access necessary to perform their job functions. This reduces the risk of unauthorized access and limits the potential impact of a security breach.

Strong Authentication: Strong authentication mechanisms, such as multi-factor authentication (MFA), should be used to verify the identity of users before granting access. This helps prevent unauthorized access to sensitive data or functionality.

Access Monitoring: Access to sensitive data or functionality should be monitored to detect and prevent unauthorized access. This can be done through the use of audit logs, intrusion detection systems and other monitoring tools.

Regular Access Reviews: Access rights should be reviewed regularly to ensure that users only have access to the resources they need. This helps ensure that access rights are up to date and reduces the risk of unauthorized access.

Segregation of Duties: Access control should be designed to prevent any one person from having too much control over a system or process. This reduces the risk of fraud or unauthorized access by preventing a single user from having too much power.

Access Control Implementation

To implement access control effectively organizations should follow a structured approach:

Define Access Control Requirements: Organizations should define their access control requirements based on their security policies, compliance requirements and risk assessments. This includes identifying the resources that need to be protected, the types of users who require access and the types of access that are required.

Select Access Control Mechanisms: Organizations should select the appropriate access control mechanisms based on their requirements. This may include RBAC, ABAC, DAC or MAC, depending on the level of security required and the complexity of the environment.

Implement Access Control Policies: Access control policies should be implemented to enforce access control mechanisms. This includes defining roles and permissions, configuring authentication mechanisms and setting up access monitoring and auditing.

Test and Evaluate: Access control mechanisms should be tested and evaluated to ensure their effectiveness in protecting websites and web applications from attacks. This can involve conducting regular security audits, vulnerability assessments and penetration testing to identify and address any weaknesses or vulnerabilities in the access control measures. Additionally, monitoring and logging mechanisms should be implemented to detect and alert on any suspicious or unauthorized access attempts in real-time. Regular testing and evaluation of access control mechanisms can help identify and address any potential gaps in security, ensuring that access is granted only to authorized users and preventing unauthorized access to sensitive data or resources.

Another important aspect of access control is the principle of least privilege, which involves granting users only the minimum level of access they need to perform their tasks. This reduces the risk of accidental or intentional misuse of resources by limiting the potential harm that can be caused by any one user. For example, a user with limited access to a system cannot accidentally delete or modify critical files, nor can they intentionally access sensitive data they should not be authorized to view.

Access control also involves authentication and authorization processes. Authentication verifies the identity of a user and ensures that they are who they claim to be. This can be achieved through a variety of methods, such as usernames and passwords, biometric authentication or multi-factor authentication. Authorization, on the other hand, determines what resources a user is allowed to access based on their identity and level of privilege.

One common method of access control is role-based access control (RBAC), which assigns permissions based on a user's job function or role within an organization. This approach simplifies the process of managing access control by grouping users into predefined roles and granting them access to the resources they need to perform their job duties.

Another approach to access control is attribute-based access control (ABAC), which takes into account a range of user attributes such as their job title, location and department. ABAC enables organizations to implement more granular access control policies by considering multiple factors when making access decisions.

Access control mechanisms can be implemented through a variety of means, including firewalls, routers and other security devices, as well as at the application and database level. It is important to regularly review and update access control policies and mechanisms to ensure that they continue to effectively protect resources from unauthorized access.

Access control is a crucial component of any online security strategy. It involves implementing policies and mechanisms that limit access to resources based on a user's identity and level of privilege, as well as following the principle of least privilege. By implementing effective access control measures organizations can reduce the risk of unauthorized access to sensitive data and prevent security breaches.

C.6.   Patch Management

One of the essential methods to protect websites and web applications from attacks is through effective patch management. It is the process of updating systems and applications to fix security vulnerabilities and prevent exploits. Regularly patching systems and applications can help prevent attacks that take advantage of known vulnerabilities.

Patch management refers to the process of regularly updating and maintaining software applications with the latest security patches released by vendors. These patches are designed to address vulnerabilities, bugs and weaknesses in the software that can be exploited by cybercriminals. By staying up to date with patches organizations can significantly reduce the risk of cyber attacks, minimize potential damages and safeguard the confidentiality, integrity and availability of their websites and web applications.

In this chapter, we will examine the intricacies of patch management as a critical component of online security. We will explore the challenges associated with patch management, best practices for implementing an effective patch management strategy and the benefits of staying proactive in keeping your software up to date.

The Importance of Patch Management

Software vendors release patches to address these vulnerabilities and protect their software from potential attacks. However, if these patches are not applied in a timely manner, websites and web applications remain vulnerable to exploitation.

Patch management is crucial for safeguarding websites and web applications for several reasons:

Vulnerability Mitigation: Cybercriminals are constantly on the lookout for vulnerabilities in popular software applications. When a vulnerability is discovered and publicly disclosed, it becomes a race against time to patch the vulnerability before it can be exploited. Patch management allows organizations to stay ahead of cyber threats by mitigating known vulnerabilities and reducing the attack surface.

Defense in Depth: Online security is a multi-layered approach and patch management is an important layer in the defense-in-depth strategy. By applying patches to software applications organizations add an additional layer of protection against potential attacks. This complements other security measures, such as firewalls, intrusion detection systems (IDS) and antivirus software, to create a robust security posture.

Compliance Requirements: Many industries and regulatory frameworks require organizations to maintain updated software applications as part of their compliance requirements. Patch management ensures that organizations meet these regulatory obligations and avoid penalties and legal consequences.

Reputation Protection: A data breach or a successful cyber attack can have severe repercussions on an organization's reputation. Customers, partners and stakeholders may lose trust in an organization's ability to protect sensitive information. Patch management helps organizations demonstrate their commitment to security and safeguard their reputation by proactively addressing known vulnerabilities.

Challenges in Patch Management

While patch management is critical for online security, it can be a complex and challenging process. Organizations face various challenges in implementing an effective patch management strategy. Let's explore some of the common challenges:

Patch Prioritization: With the multitude of software applications and vendors in use organizations may face challenges in prioritizing which patches to apply first. Not all patches are of equal importance and organizations must assess the severity and potential impact of each patch before applying them. This can be time-consuming and requires a good understanding of the organization's risk appetite and business priorities.

Patch Testing: Applying patches without proper testing can potentially disrupt software applications or cause unintended consequences. Organizations need to test patches in a controlled environment to ensure that they do not introduce new issues or conflicts with existing configurations. Testing can be resource-intensive and may require coordination between different teams, including development, operations and security, to ensure that patches are thoroughly tested before deployment.

Patch Compatibility: Organizations often use a wide range of software applications from different vendors, each with its own release cycles and compatibility requirements. Applying patches to complex software ecosystems can be challenging, as patches for one software application may conflict with another or require additional configuration changes. Ensuring patch compatibility across different software applications and environments can be time-consuming and may require careful coordination and testing.

Patch Deployment: Deploying patches across a large number of servers, systems and applications can be a daunting task. Organizations must have a well-defined and efficient process for deploying patches, including change management, rollback procedures and backup and recovery plans in case of issues during deployment. Coordination among different teams, proper scheduling and monitoring are critical to ensure that patches are deployed effectively without disrupting critical business operations.

Legacy Systems: Many organizations still rely on legacy systems and applications that may not receive regular updates and patches from vendors. These legacy systems can pose significant security risks, as they may have unaddressed vulnerabilities that can be exploited by attackers. Patching legacy systems can be challenging due to compatibility issues, lack of vendor support and potential disruption of critical business processes.

Best Practices for Patch Management

Despite the challenges organizations can implement an effective patch management strategy by following best practices. Here are some recommendations for successful patch management:

Develop a Patch Management Policy: Organizations should establish a formal patch management policy that outlines the procedures, responsibilities and timelines for applying patches. The policy should align with the organization's risk appetite, compliance requirements and business priorities. It should also include guidelines for patch prioritization, testing, deployment and rollback procedures.

Stay Informed about Vulnerabilities: Organizations should stay informed about the latest vulnerabilities and patches released by software vendors. This can be done by subscribing to vendor mailing lists, security advisories and industry news. Organizations should also establish relationships with vendor contacts and participate in security communities and forums to stay updated about emerging threats and vulnerabilities.

Perform Regular Vulnerability Assessments: Regular vulnerability assessments can help organizations identify potential vulnerabilities in their software applications and prioritize patches accordingly. Vulnerability scanning tools can scan systems and applications for known vulnerabilities and provide reports on the severity and impact of each vulnerability. This information can be used to prioritize patches based on risk assessment and criticality.

Test Patches in a Controlled Environment: Before deploying patches in production environments organizations should thoroughly test them in a controlled environment to identify any potential conflicts or issues. Testing should include functional testing, compatibility testing and security testing to ensure that patches do not introduce new vulnerabilities or disrupt critical business processes. Testing should be performed in a segregated environment that closely mimics the production environment to ensure accuracy.

Follow a Risk-Based Patching Approach: Organizations should adopt a risk-based patching approach that prioritizes patches based on their severity, impact and exploitability. Critical patches that address vulnerabilities with a high risk of exploitation should be prioritized and deployed as soon as possible, followed by patches for vulnerabilities with lower risk. A risk-based approach ensures that organizations focus their resources on addressing the most critical vulnerabilities first and minimize the potential impact of cyber attacks.

Automate Patch Deployment: Organizations should leverage automation tools and technologies to streamline the patch deployment process. Automation can help in scheduling, deploying and monitoring patches across large numbers of systems and applications, reducing human errors and ensuring consistency in patch management procedures. Automation can also help in generating reports and tracking patch compliance.

Monitor and Audit Patch Compliance: Organizations should implement monitoring and auditing mechanisms to track patch compliance and ensure that all systems and applications are up to date with the latest patches. Regular audits can help organizations identify gaps in patch management procedures and take corrective actions to address those gaps. Monitoring can involve the use of security information and event management

(SIEM) tools, log analysis and vulnerability scanning to detect any deviations from the patch management policy and promptly address them.

Keep Backup and Recovery Plans in Place: Patching can sometimes result in unexpected issues, such as system failures or application errors. Organizations should have a well-defined backup and recovery plan in place to ensure business continuity in case of any patch-related disruptions. This includes regularly backing up critical systems and applications, testing the restore process and having a plan in place for rollback procedures in case a patch deployment fails.

Educate Users and Employees: User awareness and education play a crucial role in the success of patch management. Organizations should regularly educate users and employees about the importance of patching, the risks of unpatched vulnerabilities and the role they play in maintaining a secure online environment. Training sessions, awareness campaigns and regular reminders can help in promoting a security-conscious culture within the organization.

Regularly Review and Update Patch Management Procedures: Patch management is an ongoing process that requires regular review and updates. Organizations should periodically review their patch management procedures, policies and tools to ensure that they are effective in addressing the changing threat landscape and evolving business requirements. Feedback from stakeholders, lessons learned from previous patch deployments and industry best practices should be considered for continuous improvement.

Patch management is a critical component of online security that helps organizations protect their websites and web applications from known vulnerabilities and cyber attacks. It requires a comprehensive and well-defined approach that encompasses vulnerability assessment, patch prioritization, testing, deployment, monitoring and user awareness. By following best practices organizations can ensure that their systems and applications are up to date with the latest patches, reducing the risk of security breaches and maintaining a secure online environment. Remember, patching is not a one-time task but a continuous process that requires diligence, coordination and a proactive approach to stay ahead of emerging threats and vulnerabilities. By prioritizing patch management as a fundamental part of their security strategy organizations can significantly enhance their online security posture and protect their critical assets from potential cyber threats.

III. EMAIL SECURITY

A. Overview

Email is one of the most widely used forms of communication and is essential for both personal and business use. However, with the rise of email usage has come a corresponding rise in email-based threats. Email security is essential to protect sensitive information, prevent the spread of malware and maintain the confidentiality and privacy of email communications. In this chapter, we will examine the key elements of email security and the importance of protecting email systems from threats.

A.1.   Spam and Phishing

Spam is unsolicited commercial email or unwanted email messages sent in bulk. Spam emails often contain misleading information, false advertising or fraudulent offers. They are designed to promote a product or service or to trick the recipient into clicking a link or providing personal information. Some of the common types of spam emails are:

Advertising spam: These emails contain advertisements for products or services that the recipient did not request or ask for.

Chain emails: These are emails that contain a message urging the recipient to forward the email to multiple people.

Scam emails: These are fraudulent emails that pretend to be from a legitimate source, such as a bank or a government agency and ask the recipient to provide sensitive information such as login credentials, credit card details or social security numbers.

Phishing is a type of cyber-attack that aims to steal sensitive information by masquerading as a trustworthy source. Phishing attacks typically involve sending an email that appears to be from a reputable company, organization or individual. The email often contains a link to a fake website that is designed to look like the real one. Once the user enters their login credentials or personal information, the attacker can use it for their own purposes.

Phishing emails can be very convincing and the attackers often use social engineering techniques to gain the victim's trust. They may use urgency, fear or curiosity to prompt the user to click on a link or enter their information. Some of the common types of phishing emails are:

Spear phishing: These are targeted phishing attacks that are personalized to the recipient's interests or job title.

Whaling: These are phishing attacks that target high-level executives, CEOsor other individuals with access to sensitive information.

Pharming: These are attacks that redirect the user to a fake website without their knowledge, often by manipulating the DNS or URL.

Now that we understand what spam and phishing are, let's discuss some best practices for protecting yourself from these attacks:

Use a spam filter: Most email providers have built-in spam filters that can help reduce the number of spam emails you receive. Make sure to turn on this feature and periodically review your spam folder to ensure that legitimate emails are not being marked as spam.

Be cautious of unknown senders: If you receive an email from an unknown sender, do not click on any links or open any attachments. Delete the email or mark it as spam.

Check the sender's email address: Scammers often use email addresses that look like they are from a reputable source. Check the email address carefully to ensure that it is legitimate.

Avoid clicking on links: If you receive an email with a link, hover over it to see the URL. If it looks suspicious, do not click on it. Instead, type the URL into your browser or use a search engine to find the correct website.

Check the website's security: Before entering any personal information on a website, check to see if it is secure. Look for the lock icon in the address bar and make sure that the URL starts with "https" instead of "http."

Use strong passwords: Use unique, complex passwords for each account and enable two-factor authentication whenever possible. This will help prevent attackers from accessing your accounts even if they have your password.

Educate yourself: Stay up to date on the latest spam and phishing trends and techniques by reading security blogs and news articles. Familiarize yourself with the common types of scams and how to identify them. Share this information with your friends and family so that they can also protect themselves.

Use anti-virus software: Install anti-virus software on your computer and keep it up to date. This will help detect and remove any malware that may have been installed on your system.

Be wary of urgent requests: If an email or website is urging you to take immediate action, such as providing personal information or sending money, be cautious. Scammers often use urgency to pressure victims into making hasty decisions.

Trust your instincts: If something feels off or too good to be true, it probably is. Trust your instincts and do not take any action until you have verified the authenticity of the request.

Spam and phishing attacks pose a significant threat to online security. By understanding what spam and phishing are, how they work and how to protect yourself from them, you can minimize the risk of falling victim to these attacks. Follow the best practices outlined in this chapter and stay vigilant to ensure that your online activities remain secure.

A.2.   Malware

Malwares can take many forms, including viruses, trojans, worms, spyware, adware and ransomware. Each of these types of malware has a different purpose but they all share the common goal of compromising the security of your computer system. Some of the most common types of malware that can be transmitted via email are:

Email viruses: These are viruses that are transmitted via email attachments. When the user opens the attachment, the virus is executed and it can spread to other computers via email.

Trojan horses: These are malware programs that masquerade as legitimate software. When the user installs the program, the Trojan horse can be used to gain unauthorized access to the user's computer system.

Phishing scams: Some phishing scams can include malware links or attachments. When the user clicks on the link or opens the attachment, the malware is installed on their computer.

Ransomware: This is a type of malware that encrypts the user's files and demands a ransom in exchange for the decryption key.

Now that we understand what malware is, let's discuss some best practices for protecting yourself from malware attacks:

Use anti-virus software: Install anti-virus software on your computer and keep it up to date. This will help detect and remove any malware that may have been installed on your system.

Be wary of unknown senders: If you receive an email from an unknown sender, do not click on any links or open any attachments. Delete the email or mark it as spam.

Check the sender's email address: Scammers often use email addresses that look like they are from a reputable source. Check the email address carefully to ensure that it is legitimate.

Avoid clicking on links: If you receive an email with a link, hover over it to see the URL. If it looks suspicious, do not click on it. Instead, type the URL into your browser or use a search engine to find the correct website.

Check the website's security: Before entering any personal information on a website, check to see if it is secure. Look for the lock icon in the address bar and make sure that the URL starts with "https" instead of "http."

Use strong passwords: Use unique, complex passwords for each account and enable two-factor authentication whenever possible. This will help prevent attackers from accessing your accounts even if they have your password.

Keep your software up to date: Malware often exploits vulnerabilities in software programs to gain access to your computer system. Make sure to keep your operating system and other software programs up to date with the latest security patches and updates.

Educate yourself: Stay up to date on the latest malware trends and techniques by reading security blogs and news articles. Familiarize yourself with the common types of malware and how to identify them. Share this information with your friends and family so that they can also protect themselves.

Backup your data: Regularly backup your important data to an external hard drive or a cloud-based service. This will help ensure that your files can be recovered in case of a malware attack.

Malware attacks pose a significant threat to online security. By understanding what malware is, how it Works and how to protect yourself from it, you can significantly reduce your risk of falling victim to a malware attack. Remember to always use anti-virus software, be wary of unknown senders, check the sender's email address, avoid clicking on links and check the website's security. These best practices, combined with a healthy dose of skepticism and caution can go a long way in keeping you safe from malware attacks.

A.3.   Email Encryption

As we examined before at "Methods for Protecting Networks from Attacks" chapter, email encryption is an essential tool for protecting sensitive information transmitted via email. In this section, we'll explore the basics of email encryption, how it works and why it's important.

Email encryption involves the use of mathematical algorithms to scramble the contents of an email message so that it can only be read by the intended recipient. This is accomplished by encrypting the message using a public key, which can only be decrypted by the recipient using their private key. This process ensures that even if a hacker intercepts the email, they won't be able to read its contents without the private key.

There are two main types of email encryption: S/MIME and PGP (Pretty Good Privacy). S/MIME is a widely used standard for email encryption that is built into many email clients such as Microsoft Outlook and Apple Mail. PGP, on the other hand, is a more flexible and widely used encryption protocol that can be used with a variety of email clients and platforms.

To use email encryption, you will need to obtain a digital certificate that contains your public key. This can typically be obtained from a trusted third-party provider or generated using encryption software. Once you have a digital certificate, you can then enable encryption on your email client and begin sending encrypted messages.

One of the main advantages of email encryption is that it allows you to transmit sensitive information securely. This is particularly important for businesses and organizations that deal with sensitive customer information or trade secrets. By encrypting email messages, you can ensure that only the intended recipient can read the message, reducing the risk of information theft or data breaches.

However, it's important to note that email encryption is not foolproof. There are still ways that attackers can intercept and decrypt encrypted email messages. For example, an attacker could intercept the email before it's encrypted or they could hack into the recipient's email account and gain access to their private key.

To maximize the security of your encrypted email messages, it's important to follow best practices. This includes using strong passwords to protect your digital certificate, keeping your software up to date and being careful about who you share your public key with.

In addition to using email encryption, there are other steps you can take to protect your email communications. For example, you can use secure email providers that offer end-to-end encryption, which ensures that your emails are encrypted at all times, even when they're stored on the email server.

Overall, email security is an essential aspect of protecting sensitive information and maintaining the privacy and confidentiality of email communications. Understanding the key elements of email security, including spam, phishing, malware and email encryption, is essential for organizations and individuals looking to protect their email systems from threats. In the next chapter, we will examine the methods used to protect against email-based threats and the importance of implementing email security measures.

B. Types of Email Attacks and How They Work

Email-based attacks are a growing threat to organizations and individuals and can cause significant damage to computer systems, steal sensitive information and disrupt normal business operations. In this chapter, we will examine the various types of email attacks and how they work, including phishing, malware and spear phishing.

B.1.   Phishing

Phishing is a type of online attack in which an attacker sends a fraudulent email to a victim in an attempt to trick them into divulging sensitive information, such as login credentials or credit card numbers. The email may appear to come from a legitimate source, such as a bank or an e-commerce website and often contains a link to a fake login page designed to steal the victim's credentials.

How Does Phishing Work?

Phishing attacks typically begin with an email sent to the victim. The email is designed to look like it came from a legitimate source, such as a bank or an e-commerce website. The email will often contain a link to a fake login page that is designed to look like the real thing. The victim is then prompted to enter their login credentials, which are sent directly to the attacker.

In some cases, the attacker may also use social engineering tactics to make the victim more likely to fall for the scam. For example, the email may contain a urgent request for the victim to update their account information or to change their password immediately. The attacker may also create a sense of urgency by threatening to suspend the victim's account or take other punitive measures if they do not comply.

How to Protect Yourself Against Phishing

There are several steps you can take to protect yourself against phishing attacks:

Be wary of emails from unknown senders: If you receive an email from an unfamiliar sender, be cautious about clicking any links or opening any attachments. It's possible that the email could be a phishing attempt.

Verify the sender: If you receive an email from a sender claiming to be a legitimate organization, such as a bank or an e-commerce website, verify the sender's identity before responding to the email or clicking any links. You can usually do this by checking the sender's email address, which should match the organization's domain name.

Look for warning signs: Phishing emails often contain spelling or grammatical errors or may use overly urgent language to create a sense of panic. Be on the lookout for these warning signs and take them as a red flag.

Use two-factor authentication: Many websites now offer two-factor authentication, which requires users to enter a secondary code in addition to their password. This can help protect against phishing attacks, as even if an attacker gains access to your password, they won't be able to access your account without the secondary code.

Keep your software up to date: Many phishing attacks take advantage of software vulnerabilities in order to gain access to a victim's computer or account. By keeping your software up to date, you can reduce the risk of these types of attacks.

Phishing is a serious threat that can result in significant financial loss and damage to your personal or professional reputation. By staying vigilant and taking the appropriate precautions, you can protect yourself against these types of attacks and keep your sensitive information safe.

B.2.   Malware

As we examined before, malware is a type of software designed to cause harm to computer systems. Malware can be spread through email attachments or links and can cause damage to a user's computer or steal sensitive information. Email-based malware can take many forms, including viruses, worms and Trojan horses and can be difficult to detect and remove. Once malware has been installed on a computer, it can be used to steal sensitive information, such as login credentials and financial data or to control the computer for malicious purposes.

Spear Phishing

Spear phishing is a type of phishing attack that targets specific individuals or organizations. Unlike traditional phishing attacks, which are sent to a large number of individuals, spear phishing attacks are carefully crafted to appear as though they are coming from a trusted source, such as a coworker or business partner. The attacker will often gather information about the target, such as their job title, personal interests and email addresses, to create a more convincing and targeted phishing attack.

How does spear phishing work?

Spear phishing works by sending a targeted email that appears to come from a trusted source, such as a colleague, friend or family member. The email may contain a link to a malicious website, a file attachment that contains malware or a request for sensitive information, such as passwords or credit card numbers.

The email is carefully crafted to look legitimate and to create a sense of urgency or fear in the recipient. For example, the email may claim that the recipient's bank account has been compromised and that they need to enter their account details immediately to prevent further damage.

Once the recipient clicks on the link or opens the attachment, the malware is downloaded onto their computer. The malware can then be used to steal sensitive information, such as passwords, credit card numbers and personal data.

Why is spear phishing so effective?

Spear phishing is so effective because it is personalized and targeted towards specific individuals or groups. The email appears to come from a trusted source and may contain information that only the recipient would know. This creates a sense of trust and makes the recipient more likely to click on the link or open the attachment.

In addition, spear phishing attacks are often timed to coincide with specific events, such as holidays or major news events. This increases the likelihood that the recipient will be distracted or preoccupied and less likely to scrutinize the email carefully.

How to protect against spear phishing?

There are several steps that individuals and organizations can take to protect themselves against spear phishing attacks.

Education: One of the most effective ways to protect against spear phishing attacks is to educate individuals about the risks and how to identify phishing emails. This includes training employees on how to recognize suspicious emails, how to check the authenticity of an email and how to report suspected phishing attempts.

Two-factor authentication: Implementing two-factor authentication for sensitive accounts can help prevent unauthorized access even if the attacker has obtained the user's password.

Anti-malware software: Installing anti-malware software on all devices can help prevent malware from being downloaded onto the device.

Use of spam filters: Implementing spam filters can help block suspicious emails before they reach the recipient's inbox.

Regular software updates: Regularly updating software can help prevent vulnerabilities that could be exploited by attackers.

Use of encryption: Using encryption for sensitive data can help prevent attackers from intercepting and stealing data.

Spear phishing is a highly effective form of email attack that can cause significant damage to individuals and organizations. However, by taking the necessary precautions, individuals and organizations can protect themselves against spear phishing attacks. Education, two-factor authentication, anti-malware software, spam filters, regular software updates and encryption are all important steps in protecting against spear phishing attacks.

Email-based attacks are a growing threat to organizations and individuals and can cause significant damage to computer systems, steal sensitive information and disrupt normal business operations. Understanding the various types of email attacks and how they work, including phishing, malware and spear phishing is essential for organizations and individuals looking to protect their email systems from threats. In the next chapter, we will examine the methods used to protect against email-based threats and the importance of implementing email security measures.

C. Methods for Protecting Email Systems from Attacks

Email-based attacks are a growing threat to organizations and individuals and it is important to take steps to protect email systems from these threats. In this chapter, we will examine the methods used to protect against email-based threats and the importance of implementing email security measures.

C.1.   Anti-Virus and Anti-Malware Software

One of the most effective ways to protect against email-based threats is to install and regularly update anti-virus and anti-malware software. This software is designed to detect and remove malicious software, such as viruses, worms and Trojan horses, before they can cause damage to computer systems. Anti-virus and anti-malware software can be configured to scan incoming email messages and attachments and to remove any detected threats.

C.2.   Email Filtering

Another effective method for protecting email systems from attacks is to implement email filtering. Email filtering software can be configured to identify and block email messages that contain malicious attachments or links or that appear to be from suspicious or unknown sources. This software can also be configured to block messages that contain certain keywords or phrases or that match certain patterns associated with spam or phishing attacks.

Why is email filtering important?

Email filtering is important for several reasons. First, email is a primary method of communication for most organizations and therefore it is a prime target for attackers. Malicious emails can contain viruses, malwareor other forms of malicious code that can infect the recipient's device or network.

Second, email filtering can help prevent phishing attacks. Phishing attacks are a common type of email attack that are designed to trick the recipient into revealing sensitive information, such as login credentials or financial data. By filtering out phishing emails before they reach the recipient organizations can significantly reduce the risk of a successful attack.

Third, email filtering can help prevent spam. Spam is unsolicited email that is sent in bulk. It is often used to distribute malware or phishing emails. By filtering out spam organizations can reduce the amount of time and resources spent on managing unwanted emails.

Types of email filtering

There are several types of email filtering that organizations can use to protect their email systems from attacks.

Content filtering: Content filtering is the process of analyzing the content of an email to identify potentially malicious or unwanted content. This can include analyzing the text of the email, attachments and embedded links.

Attachment filtering: Attachment filtering is the process of analyzing email attachments to identify potentially malicious files, such as executable files, scripts and macros.

Sender filtering: Sender filtering is the process of analyzing the sender's email address to identify potentially malicious senders. This can include blocking emails from known spam senders or blocking emails from certain countries or regions.

Reputation filtering: Reputation filtering is the process of analyzing the reputation of the sender's IP address or domain. This can include blocking emails from known sources of spam or malware.

Behavioral filtering: Behavioral filtering is the process of analyzing the behavior of the email recipient to identify potentially malicious emails. For example, if an email is sent to multiple recipients who do not typically communicate with each other, it may be flagged as potentially malicious.

How to implement email filtering

Implementing email filtering requires a combination of technology, policies and procedures. Here are some steps that organizations can take to implement effective email filtering:

Define filtering policies: Organizations should define policies for filtering emails based on certain criteria, such as sender, subject line, content and attachment type. These policies should be based on the organization's security requirements and risk profile.

Choose a filtering solution: Organizations can choose from a variety of email filtering solutions, including cloud-based solutions and on-premises solutions. The solution should be able to filter emails based on the defined policies and provide alerts or reports on potentially malicious emails.

Train employees: Employees should be trained on how to identify potentially malicious emails and how to report them to the IT department. This can include training on how to recognize phishing emails, how to check the authenticity of an email and how to report suspected phishing attempts.

Test the filtering solution: Organizations should regularly test their email filtering solution to ensure that it is effective in identifying and blocking potentially malicious emails. This can include testing the solution against known malware and phishing emails.

In conclusion, email filtering is a critical method for protecting email systems from attacks. By implementing effective email filtering and taking other steps to protect email systems organizations can significantly reduce the risk of a successful email attack. However, it is important to recognize that email attacks are constantly evolving and organizations must remain vigilant and proactive in their approach to email security.

C.3. Email Authentication

Email authentication is a method for verifying the identity of the sender of an email message. It is an essential component of email security, as it can help prevent email spoofing and other forms of email-based attacks.

Email authentication works by using various authentication mechanisms to validate that the email message has come from the sender it claims to be from. These mechanisms include:

Sender Policy Framework (SPF): SPF is an email authentication mechanism that allows the owner of a domain to specify which IP addresses are authorized to send email messages from that domain. SPF works by publishing a list of authorized IP addresses in the domain's DNS records. When an email message is received, the recipient's email server checks the SPF record to verify that the IP address of the sending server is authorized to send email from the sender's domain.

DomainKeys Identified Mail (DKIM): DKIM is an email authentication mechanism that adds a digital signature to the email message header to verify that the message has not been tampered with during transit. The digital signature is created using a private key that is stored on the sender's email server and the recipient's email server uses the public key, which is published in the sender's DNS records, to verify the signature.

Domain-based Message Authentication, Reportingand Conformance (DMARC): DMARC is an email authentication protocol that uses SPF and DKIM to provide a comprehensive email authentication solution. DMARC allows the domain owner to specify how the recipient's email server should handle email messages that fail SPF or DKIM checks. DMARC also provides reporting capabilities that allow domain owners to monitor and analyze email traffic.

By using these email authentication mechanisms organizations can significantly reduce the risk of email-based attacks, such as phishing and spoofing. However, it is important to note that email authentication is not foolproof and attackers can still find ways to circumvent it. Therefore, it is important to implement other email security measures, such as email filtering and employee education, to provide a comprehensive email security solution.

Implementing email authentication can also have other benefits beyond security. For example, it can help improve email deliverability by reducing the likelihood that legitimate email messages will be marked as spam. Email authentication can also help organizations build trust with their customers by demonstrating that they are taking steps to protect their email communications.

Email authentication is an essential component of email security. By implementing SPF, DKIMand DMARCorganizations can significantly reduce the risk of email-based attacks and improve email deliverability. However, it is important to recognize that email authentication is just one piece of the email security puzzle and organizations must take a comprehensive approach to email security to effectively protect their email systems.

C.4.   User Awareness and Training

One of the most important things that organizations can do to protect their email systems is to educate users on best practices. This includes:

- Avoiding clicking on suspicious links or opening attachments from unknown sources
- Verifying the sender's email address before responding to or clicking on any links within an email
- Using strong passwords and changing them regularly
- Enabling two-factor authentication to add an extra layer of security
- Keeping software and security systems up to date
- Reporting any suspicious activity to IT or security personnel

C.5.   Monitoring and Responding to Email Threats

Even with the best education and tools in place, it is still possible for email threats to slip through the cracks. That's why it is important to have a plan in place for monitoring and responding to these threats. This may include:

- Regularly monitoring email traffic for signs of suspicious activity
- Having a plan in place for responding to potential threats, including identifying the source of the threat, containing the damage and notifying affected parties
- Conducting regular security audits and vulnerability assessments to identify potential weaknesses in the email system
- Keeping up to date with the latest threats and trends in email security and adjusting security measures accordingly

Protecting email systems from attacks is a complex and ongoing process that requires a combination of education, tools and vigilance. By educating users on best practices, providing them with the tools they need to stay safe and monitoring and responding to potential threats organizations can help minimize the risk of a successful attack.

IV. DATA SECURITY

A. Overview

Data security is the practice of protecting sensitive information from unauthorized access, use, disclosure, disruption, modification or destruction. Data security is becoming increasingly important, as individuals and organizations alike are storing more sensitive information electronically. In this chapter, we will provide an overview of data security and its importance.

A.1. Types of Sensitive Information

Sensitive information can come in many forms, including personal information, financial information, trade secrets and more. The importance of protecting this information can vary but it is always important to take appropriate measures to prevent unauthorized access, use or disclosure.

A.2. Data Security Threats

There are many different types of threats to data security, including unauthorized access, theft, loss and destruction. These threats can come from a variety of sources, including malicious insiders, external attackers and natural disasters.

A.3. Importance of Data Security

Data security is important for several reasons, including:

Protecting sensitive information from unauthorized access, use or disclosure.

Preventing loss or theft of sensitive information.

Maintaining the confidentiality, integrity and availability of sensitive information.

Complying with legal and regulatory requirements, such as privacy laws and data protection regulations.

Protecting the reputation and brand of an organization.

Data Security Standards and Regulations

To help organizations protect sensitive information, there are a number of data security standards and regulations that organizations can follow. Some examples of these standards and regulations include the Payment Card Industry Data Security Standard (PCI DSS), the Health Insurance Portability and Accountability Act (HIPAA) and the General Data Protection Regulation (GDPR).

Data security is an important issue for individuals and organizations alike and it is important to be aware of the types of data security threats and how they can be prevented. In the next chapter, we will examine the steps that organizations can take to protect their sensitive information and maintain a secure data environment.

B. Types of Data Security Threats and How They Work

Data security threats come in many forms and can come from a variety of sources, including malicious insiders, external attackers and natural disasters. We will provide a summary for some of the topics in this section as they have been extensively discussed in previous sections but we will delve into the topic of ransomware in detail.

B.1.   Malware

Malware is malicious software that is designed to cause harm to a computer system. This can include viruses, worms and Trojans, among others. Malware can infect a computer system through a variety of means, including email attachments, infected software and drive-by downloads from infected websites.

B.2.   Phishing

Phishing is a type of social engineering attack that uses email or other electronic communication to trick individuals into revealing sensitive information. Phishing attacks often take the form of emails that appear to be from a legitimate source, such as a financial institution but are actually from attackers who are attempting to steal sensitive information.

B.3.   Man-in-the-Middle Attacks

Man-in-the-middle attacks occur when an attacker intercepts and manipulates communication between two parties. This can include intercepting sensitive information, such as login credentials and manipulating the communication in order to steal sensitive information or cause harm to a computer system.

B.4   Ransomware

In recent years, ransomware has emerged as one of the most prevalent and dangerous cyber threats to individuals and organizations alike. Ransomware is a type of malware that encrypts a victim's data and demands a ransom payment in exchange for the decryption key. In this chapter, we will explore the various types of ransomware and the methods used to infect systems, as well as steps that can be taken to prevent and mitigate the damage caused by ransomware attacks.

Types of Ransomware:

There are two main types of ransomware: crypto ransomware and locker ransomware. Crypto ransomware is the most common type and encrypts a victim's data, rendering it inaccessible until the ransom is paid. Locker ransomware, on the other hand, locks the victim out of their system by changing the login credentials or locking the screen.

In addition to these two main types, there are also hybrid ransomware strains that combine the features of both crypto and locker ransomware. These hybrid strains may encrypt the victim's data and then lock them out of their system.

Crypto Ransomware

Crypto ransomware encrypts the victim's files and demands a ransom payment in exchange for the decryption key. The term "crypto" refers to the encryption algorithms used by the malware to encrypt the victim's files, making them unreadable and inaccessible.

The process of encryption involves converting the original data into an unreadable format, known as ciphertext, using a complex mathematical algorithm. The encryption algorithm used by crypto ransomware is typically very strong and almost impossible to break without the decryption key. The decryption key is typically held by the cybercriminals who created the ransomware and they will demand a ransom payment in exchange for the key.

Once a victim's files have been encrypted, they will be presented with a ransom note, typically in the form of a pop-up window or text file which will explain the terms of the ransom. The ransom note will typically contain instructions on how to pay the ransom and obtain the decryption key. The ransom amount demanded by cybercriminals varies widely but it is often in the range of thousands of dollars.

The most common way that crypto ransomware infects systems is through phishing emails. Cybercriminals will send emails to unsuspecting victims that contain a malicious attachment or a link to a website that contains the malware. Once the victim clicks on the attachment or visits the website, the ransomware will be installed on their system. We examined phishing emails in the previous chapters.

Crypto ransomware typically uses advanced encryption algorithms such as AES (Advanced Encryption Standard) or RSA (Rivest-Shamir-Adleman) to encrypt the victim's files. AES is a symmetric encryption algorithm, meaning that the same key is used for both encryption and decryption. RSA, on the other hand, is an asymmetric encryption algorithm that uses two keys, a public key and a private key, for encryption and decryption respectively. The ransomware will typically use a combination of both symmetric and asymmetric encryption to encrypt the victim's files. First the ransomware will generate a unique symmetric key for each file that it encrypts. It will then encrypt the symmetric key using the victim's public key which is then stored along with the encrypted files. When the victim pays the ransom and obtains the decryption key, the ransomware will use the victim's private key to decrypt the symmetric key which can then be used to decrypt the encrypted files.

The encryption process used by crypto ransomware is typically very strong. However, some types of ransomware may have vulnerabilities that can be exploited to recover the decryption key without paying the ransom. In some cases, law enforcement agencies or cybersecurity researchers may be able to obtain the decryption key through various means such as reverse-engineering the ransomware code or tracking down the cybercriminals behind the attack.

Locker Ransomware

Locker ransomware is a type of malware that locks the victim out of their computer or mobile device by preventing them from accessing their files or operating system. The malware typically displays a message on the victim's screen, demanding a ransom payment in exchange for the decryption key or the removal of the locker.

Locker ransomware is different from crypto ransomware, which encrypts the victim's files rather than locking them. While crypto ransomware targets specific files, locker ransomware can lock the entire system, preventing the victim from accessing any of their files or data.

The most common way that locker ransomware infects systems is through malicious websites or email attachments. Once the malware is installed on the victim's system, it will lock the system or files and display a message demanding the ransom payment. The ransom amount demanded by cybercriminals can vary widely but is typically in the range of hundreds of dollars.

Locker ransomware works by modifying the victim's system settings or configuration files, effectively locking them out of their system or files. The malware typically uses advanced techniques to gain access to the victim's system, such as exploiting vulnerabilities in software or using social engineering techniques to trick the victim into installing the malware.

Once the malware has gained access to the victim's system, it will modify system settings or configuration files to lock the system or files. The malware may modify the boot sector of the victim's hard drive, preventing the system from booting up properly. Alternatively it may modify the Windows registry or system files, preventing the victim from accessing their files or operating system.

To unlock the system or files, the victim is typically required to pay a ransom payment. The ransomware message will typically contain instructions on how to pay the ransom which is typically in the form of cryptocurrency such as Bitcoin.

Preventing locker ransomware requires a combination of good security practices and user awareness. Some best practices for preventing locker ransomware include:

Keeping software up to date: Ensuring that operating systems, software applicationsand security software are up to date with the latest security patches and updates.

Using anti-malware software: Installing and using anti-malware software to detect and remove malicious software from the system.

Regularly backing up data: Regularly backing up important data to an external hard drive or cloud storage service can help to mitigate the damage caused by ransomware attacks.

Being vigilant against phishing attacks: Being aware of phishing attacks and not clicking on suspicious links or downloading attachments from unknown sources.

Educating employees: Educating employees about the risks of ransomware and the importance of good security practices can help to prevent ransomware attacks.

Hybrid Ransomware

Hybrid ransomware is a type of malware that combines features of both crypto ransomware and locker ransomware. These types of ransomware attacks can be particularly damaging as they can lock the victim out of their system and encrypt their files simultaneously.

In a hybrid ransomware attack, the malware first gains access to the victim's system, typically through a phishing email or malicious website. Once the malware is installed on the victim's system, it will first lock the system or files to prevent the victim from accessing them. Then, it will encrypt the victim's files, making them inaccessible and demanding a ransom payment in exchange for the decryption key.

This type of ransomware can be especially difficult to detect and prevent as it combines two different types of malware into one attack. Victims of hybrid ransomware attacks are faced with the double threat of being locked out of their system and losing access to their files.

Hybrid ransomware works by using advanced techniques to gain access to the victim's system and then executing a series of malicious activities to lock the system or files and encrypt the victim's data. The malware typically uses sophisticated encryption algorithms such as AES-256 to encrypt the victim's files, making them virtually impossible to decrypt without the correct decryption key.

One of the ways that hybrid ransomware can lock the victim's system is by modifying the boot sector of the victim's hard drive, preventing the system from booting up properly. Alternatively, it may modify the Windows registry or system files, preventing the victim from accessing their files or operating system.

While we're at it, let's also talk about modifying the hard drive boot sector.

The boot sector of a hard drive is the section of the disk that contains the code necessary to boot up the operating system. A ransomware can modify the boot sector to lock the victim's system by overwriting the original boot code with its own malicious one. When the system is restarted, it will load the malicious code instead of the original boot code, preventing the system from booting up properly.

The technical method of modifying the boot sector by ransomware involves using low-level disk access to write the malicious code to the boot sector. This requires the malware to have administrator-level access to the victim's system.

Once the malware gains administrator-level access, it will overwrite the original boot code. The malware will then typically make a backup of the original boot code and store it in another location on the disk, so that it can restore it later if necessary.

When the victim restarts their computer, the malware's malicious code will be executed instead of the original boot code. This will cause the system to become locked, displaying a message demanding a ransom payment to unlock the system.

To remove the malicious code from the boot sector can be time-consuming and costly, making it important to take steps to prevent hybrid ransomware attacks in the first place.

Overall, modifying the boot sector is a sophisticated technique that requires a high degree of technical knowledge and skill. It highlights the level of sophistication that cybercriminals are using in their ransomware attacksand emphasizes the need for organizations and individuals to take online security seriously to prevent these types of attacks.

Preventing hybrid ransomware requires a combination of good security practices and user awareness. Some best practices for preventing hybrid ransomware include:

Keeping software up to date: Ensuring that operating systems, software applicationsand security software are up to date with the latest security patches and updates.

Using anti-malware software: Installing and using anti-malware software to detect and remove malicious software from the system.

Regularly backing up data: Regularly backing up important data to an external hard drive or cloud storage service can help to mitigate the damage caused by ransomware attacks.

Being vigilant against phishing attacks: Being aware of phishing attacks and not clicking on suspicious links or downloading attachments from unknown sources.

Educating employees: Educating employees about the risks of ransomware and the importance of good security practices can help to prevent ransomware attacks.

Methods of Infection:

Ransomware can infect a system through a variety of methods, including:

Email phishing: This is one of the most common methods of ransomware infection. Cybercriminals send emails that contain malicious links or attachments that, when clicked or opened, download and install ransomware onto the victim's system.

Malicious websites: Cybercriminals may create websites that contain malicious code that can infect a victim's system when they visit the site.

Exploiting vulnerabilities: Cybercriminals may exploit known vulnerabilities in a victim's operating system or software to gain access to their system and install ransomware.

Remote Desktop Protocol (RDP) attacks: Cybercriminals may use methods to gain access to a victim's system via RDP and install ransomware. RDP attacks are a very dangerous situation that should be taken seriously. To elaborate on this topic:

RDP attacks are a type of cyber attack that target the Remote Desktop Protocol which is used to remotely access and control a computer over a network connection. These attacks can take many forms, including brute-force attacks, password-guessing attacks or man-in-the-middle attacks.

Brute-force attacks are one of the most common types of RDP attacks. In this type of attack, the attacker attempts to guess the login credentials for a remote desktop session by trying many different username and password combinations. The attacker may use automated tools to try thousands or even millions of different combinations in a short period of time. That's called a brute-force.

Password-guessing attacks are similar to brute-force attacksbut instead of trying many different combinations, the attacker may use information they have gathered about the victim to try to guess their password. For example, if the victim has used a weak password that is based on personal information such as their name or birthdate, the attacker may be able to guess it.

Man-in-the-middle attacks are more complex and sophisticated. In this type of attack, the attacker intercepts the network traffic between the victim and the remote desktop server and then uses this access to modify or redirect the traffic. This allows the attacker to steal the victim's login credentials or to control the remote desktop session.

To carry out a MitM attack, the attacker must first position themselves between the victim and the remote desktop server. This can be done by exploiting vulnerabilities in the network infrastructure or by using a rogue access point. Once the attacker has positioned themselves correctly, they can begin intercepting the network traffic.

One way that a MITM attacker can intercept network traffic is by using a tool like Wireshark to capture and analyze packets of data as they travel between the victim and the remote desktop server. This allows the attacker to see the contents of the traffic, including any login credentials that are transmitted in plaintext.

Once the attacker has intercepted the traffic, they can use this access to modify or redirect the traffic. For example, they may modify a packet to include their own login credentials instead of the victim's, allowing them to gain access to the remote desktop session. Alternatively they may redirect the traffic to a different server entirely, allowing them to carry out further attacks or steal sensitive data.

There are several effective measures that organizations and individuals can take to prevent MitM attacks. One important step is to use encryption to protect all network traffic. This can be done by using secure protocols like Transport Layer Security (TLS) or by using a virtual private network (VPN) to create a secure, encrypted tunnel for all traffic.

Another important step is to use strong authentication methods, such as two-factor authentication (2FA) or biometric authentication. This makes it much more difficult for attackers to gain access to a remote desktop session even if they are able to intercept the traffic.

It's important to regularly monitor network traffic for signs of suspicious activity. This can include looking for unusual network activity or connections to unknown servers. By detecting and responding to these threats early, damage caused by MITM attacks can prevent or minimize.

Also, one important step is to use strong and complex passwords for all accounts, including remote desktop accounts. Passwords should be a minimum of 16 characters in length and should include a mix of uppercase and lowercase letters, numbers and symbols.

Finally, it's important to limit access to remote desktop sessions to only those who need it. This can help reduce the attack surface and make it more difficult for attackers to gain access to sensitive systems and data.

Prevention and Mitigation

Preventing ransomware attacks requires a multi-layered approach, including the following steps:

Educate users: Educate employees and users about the risks of ransomware and how to identify and avoid phishing emails and malicious websites.

Keep software up to date: Install software updates and security patches as soon as they become available to prevent cybercriminals from exploiting known vulnerabilities.

Use anti-malware software: Install and use anti-malware software on all systems and devices to detect and block ransomware infections.

Use strong passwords: Encourage users to use strong passwords and two-factor authentication to prevent cybercriminals from accessing their systems via RDP.

Regularly backup data: Regularly backup all critical data to a secure, offsite location to mitigate the damage caused by ransomware attacks. This allows organizations to restore their data without paying the ransom.

In the event of a ransomware attack, the following steps can be taken to mitigate the damage:

Disconnect from the network: Immediately disconnect the infected system from the network to prevent the ransomware from spreading to other systems.

Don't pay the ransom: Paying the ransom does not guarantee that the data will be decrypted. Also it encourages attackers to continue their activities.

Restore data from backups: Restore all critical data from backups to recover from the ransomware attack.

Data security threats are a constant concern for individuals and organizations and it is important to be aware of the types of threats that exist and how they work. In the next chapter, we will examine some of the steps that people can take to protect their sensitive information and prevent data security incidents.

C. Methods for Protecting Sensitive Data from Unauthorized Access and Theft

Protecting sensitive data from unauthorized access and theft is a critical concern for individuals and organizations. In this chapter, we will examine some of the methods that can be used to protect sensitive data and prevent data breaches.

C.1. Encryption

As we know, encryption is the process of converting plain text into a coded format that can only be deciphered with the correct key. Encrypting sensitive data makes it unreadable to unauthorized parties and helps to prevent data breaches. There are various types of encryption algorithms, including symmetric encryption and asymmetric encryption, each with its own strengths and weaknesses.

Using full disk encryption is a security measure that involves encrypting all the data stored on a computer's hard drive or storage device. This encryption ensures that the data is protected and unreadable to anyone who doesn't have the encryption key or passphrase.

C.2. Access Control

As we discussed before, access control is the process of controlling who has access to sensitive data. This can include the use of usernames and passwords, as well as more advanced methods such as multi-factor authentication and biometric authentication. Access control systems can be used to restrict access to sensitive data to only those individuals who need it, thereby reducing the risk of data breaches.

C.3. Firewalls

We have previously explained firewalls in detail. They are network security systems that act as a barrier between a computer network and the internet. They are designed to block unauthorized access to a network and can be used to protect sensitive data from external threats.

C.4. Regular Backups

Regular backups are critical to protecting sensitive data in the event of a data breach or other security incident. Backups should be stored in a secure location and should be updated on a regular basis to ensure that the most recent version of sensitive data is always available.

C.5. Data Loss Prevention (DLP)

DLP systems are designed to prevent sensitive data from being lost, stolenor exposed. These systems use a combination of technologies and policies to detect and prevent unauthorized access, useand transmission of sensitive data.

One common method used by DLP systems is content inspection. This involves analyzing data as it travels across the network, looking for sensitive information such as social security numbers, credit card numbersor other personally identifiable information. DLP systems can use a variety of techniques to inspect content, including keyword matching, regular expressionsand machine learning algorithms.

Also, DLP systems can use a variety of access control mechanisms, such as role-based access control, attribute-based access controland multi-factor authentication.

In addition, DLP systems can also use data encryption to protect sensitive data. This makes it much more difficult for attackers to steal or view sensitive data.

DLP systems can also provide monitoring and auditing capabilities, allowing organizations to track and report on data access and usage. This can help organizations identify potential data breaches and take corrective action before sensitive data is lost or stolen.

Finally, DLP systems can include incident response and reporting features, allowing organizations to quickly respond to and report on data breaches. This can help organizations comply with data privacy regulations and minimize the impact of data loss incidents.

Protecting sensitive data from unauthorized access and theft requires a multi-layered approach that includes encryption, access control, firewalls, DLP systems and regular backups. By implementing these and other data security measures, people can reduce the risk of data breaches and protect their sensitive information.

V. CLOUD SECURITY

A. Overview

Cloud computing has revolutionized the way businesses and individuals store and access data. The ability to store and access data from anywhere in the world, at any time, has made the cloud a valuable asset for organizations of all sizes. However, as the use of cloud computing has grown, so too has the concern over its security.

In this chapter, we will explore the security concerns associated with cloud computing and the methods used to protect data stored in the cloud.

What is Cloud Security?

Cloud security is the set of measures taken to protect data stored in the cloud from unauthorized access and theft. This includes measures taken by cloud service providers, as well as measures taken by organizations that use the cloud. Cloud security is essential for organizations of all sizes because of the sensitive information that is often stored in the cloud.

A.1.   Cloud Security Concerns

There are several security concerns associated with cloud computing, including:

Data breaches: Data breaches can result in the theft of sensitive information stored in the cloud. This can have serious consequences, including financial loss and reputational damage.

Insider threats: Insider threats refer to threats that come from within an organization. This can include employees or contractors who have access to sensitive information stored in the cloud.

Malicious software: Malicious software, such as viruses and malware, can be introduced into cloud systems, which can result in the theft of sensitive information.

Data loss: Data loss can occur when data stored in the cloud is lost or corrupted. This can have serious consequences for organizations that rely on the cloud to store important information.

Methods for Protecting Data in the Cloud
There are several methods for protecting data stored in the cloud, including:

Encryption: Encryption is the process of converting plain text into an unreadable form. Encryption is used to protect data stored in the cloud by making it unreadable to unauthorized users.

Access control: Access control is the process of granting or denying access to resources, including data stored in the cloud. Access control is essential for protecting sensitive information from unauthorized access.

Monitoring and Logging: Monitoring and logging are used to track and analyze cloud activity, which can help organizations detect security threats and respond to them quickly.

Multi-factor authentication: Multi-factor authentication is a security process that requires users to provide two or more forms of authentication before accessing sensitive information stored in the cloud.

A.2.   Choosing a Cloud Service Provider

When choosing a cloud service provider, it is important to consider the security measures that the provider has in place. Organizations should look for providers that have strong security policies, regularly update their security measures and provide transparency into their security processes.

Cloud security is an important concern for organizations of all sizes. By understanding the security concerns associated with cloud computing and the methods used to protect data stored in the cloud organizations can make informed decisions about the use of cloud computing and take steps to reduce the risk of security incidents. With the right security measures in place organizations can confidently store and access data in the cloud, knowing that their sensitive information is protected.

B. Types of Cloud Security Threats and How They Work

As more and more organizations adopt cloud computing, cloud security has become a critical concern. Cloud security refers to the protection of sensitive data and systems that are hosted on remote servers managed by third-party service providers. In this chapter, we'll explore the different types of cloud security threats and how they work.

B.1. Data Breaches

A data breach occurs when an unauthorized person gains access to confidential information. This can include personal data such as names, addresses, social security numbers and credit card details, as well as business data such as financial records, intellectual propertyand trade secrets.

Data breaches can occur through various means, including hacking, phishing, malwareand social engineering. Hackers may exploit vulnerabilities in software or use brute force attacks to gain access to data. Phishing attacks involve tricking users into divulging their login credentials through emails, social mediaor other means. Malware can infect systems and steal data or allow hackers to gain remote access. Social engineering involves manipulating individuals into revealing confidential information through persuasion or coercion.

How Data Breaches Occur

Data breaches can occur through various vectors, including cloud service providers, third-party vendorsand internal systems. Cloud service providers are particularly vulnerable as they store large amounts of data for multiple customers. If a provider's security measures are insufficient, it can leave data exposed to attackers.

Third-party vendors can also be a weak point in cloud security. Many organizations rely on third-party providers for services such as data analytics, customer managementand supply chain management. If a vendor is hacked, it can compromise data for multiple organizations.

Internal systems are also vulnerable to data breaches. Employees with access to confidential data can be a source of leaks or can inadvertently expose data through security lapses such as weak passwords or unsecured devices.

Impact of Data Breaches

Data breaches can have severe consequences for individuals and organizations. In addition to financial losses, data breaches can damage reputations and lead to legal liabilities. Businesses may lose customers and suffer from diminished brand value. Individuals may experience identity theft or financial fraud.

Preventing Data Breaches

Preventing data breaches requires a comprehensive approach that involves multiple layers of security measures. Some key steps that businesses and individuals can take to protect themselves from data breaches include:

Implementing strong passwords and multi-factor authentication: Passwords should be complex and unique for each accountand multi-factor authentication should be used whenever possible.

Keeping software up to date: Software vulnerabilities can be exploited by hackers, so keeping software updated with security patches is essential.

Encrypting sensitive data: Encryption can make it more difficult for hackers to access data even if they gain unauthorized access.

Limiting access to confidential data: Access to confidential data should be restricted to authorized personnel only.

Training employees on security best practices: Employees should be educated on how to recognize and respond to security threats such as phishing attacks and malware infections.

Regularly backing up data: Regular data backups can ensure that data can be recovered in case of a breach or other disaster.

Data breaches are a serious threat to cloud securityand businesses and individuals must take steps to protect themselves from such threats. By implementing strong security measures and staying vigilant, it is possible to minimize the risk of data breaches and safeguard sensitive data.

B.2.   Insider Threats

In the world of online security, insider threats are one of the most challenging issues to address. An insider threat occurs when an individual with authorized access to an organization's data or systems intentionally or unintentionally causes harm. Insider threats can come in many forms including employees, contractors, vendors and partners. In this section we will discuss the different types of insider threats, their causes and the steps that organizations can take to mitigate these threats.

Types of Insider Threats

There are four main types of insider threats: accidental, negligent, malicious and compromised.

Accidental insider threats occur when an employee or contractor inadvertently causes harm. This can happen when they accidentally delete or corrupt data or mistakenly share confidential information.

Negligent insider threats occur when an employee or contractor fails to follow security policies or best practices. This can include using weak passwords, sharing login credentialsor failing to update software.

Malicious insider threats occur when an employee or contractor intentionally causes harm to the organization. This can include stealing sensitive data, sabotaging systemsor spreading malware.

Compromised insider threats occur when an employee or contractor's credentials are compromised by an external attacker. This can happen through phishing attacks or other social engineering techniques.

Causes of Insider Threats

There are several factors that can contribute to insider threats. These include:

Lack of security awareness: Many insider threats occur because employees or contractors are not aware of the security risks associated with their actions.

Financial gain: Some insiders may be motivated by financial gain, such as stealing trade secrets or intellectual property.

Revenge: Disgruntled employees may seek revenge against their employer by causing harm to the organization.

Negligence: Careless employees or contractors may inadvertently cause harm to the organization through their actions.

External pressure: Insiders may be coerced or manipulated by external actors to cause harm to the organization.

Mitigating Insider Threats

Mitigating insider threats requires a multi-layered approach that includes both technical and non-technical measures. Some key steps that organizations can take to mitigate insider threats include:

Access control: Organizations should implement strong access controls to ensure that employees and contractors only have access to the data and systems they need to perform their job functions.

Monitoring: Organizations should monitor employee and contractor behavior to detect unusual or suspicious activity.

Education and awareness: Organizations should educate employees and contractors on the risks associated with insider threats and how to prevent them.

Strong security policies: Organizations should implement strong security policies that include password requirements, data encryptionand regular software updates.

Incident response plan: Organizations should have an incident response plan in place to quickly respond to and contain insider threats.

Insider threats are a significant challenge for organizations of all sizes. They can cause significant harm to an organization's reputation, financesand intellectual property. However, by implementing a multi-layered approach that includes access control, monitoring, education and awareness, strong security policies and an incident response planorganizations can mitigate the risks associated with insider threats and protect their sensitive data and systems.

B.3.   Account Hijacking

Account hijacking is a type of online security threat that occurs when an attacker gains unauthorized access to a user's account. In the context of cloud security, account hijacking can be particularly damaging, as it can provide attackers with access to sensitive data and systems. In this section, we will discuss the different types of account hijacking attacks, their causesand the steps that organizations can take to mitigate these threats.

Types of Account Hijacking Attacks

There are several types of account hijacking attacks, including:

Password attacks: Password attacks involve an attacker attempting to guess or crack a user's password. This can be done through brute force attacks, dictionary attacksor social engineering.

Phishing attacks: Phishing attacks involve an attacker tricking a user into revealing their login credentials through a fake login page or email.

Malware attacks: Malware attacks involve an attacker infecting a user's computer or device with malware that can steal login credentials or take control of the user's account.

Session hijacking: Session hijacking involves an attacker intercepting a user's session token or cookie to gain access to the user's account.

Causes of Account Hijacking Attacks

Account hijacking attacks can be caused by a variety of factors, including:

Weak passwords: Weak passwords that are easily guessable or can be cracked through brute force attacks are a common cause of account hijacking.

Lack of security awareness: Users who are not aware of the risks associated with account hijacking may fall victim to phishing attacks or other social engineering tactics.

Unsecured devices: Devices that are not properly secured with up to date antivirus software and firewalls can be vulnerable to malware attacks.

Vulnerable web applications: Web applications that are not properly secured can be vulnerable to session hijacking attacks.

Mitigating Account Hijacking Attacks

Mitigating account hijacking attacks requires a multi-layered approach that includes both technical and non-technical measures. Some key steps that organizations can take to mitigate account hijacking attacks include:

Strong authentication: Organizations should implement strong authentication methods such as two-factor authentication or biometric authentication to reduce the risk of password attacks.

Security awareness training: Organizations should provide security awareness training to employees and users to help them recognize and avoid phishing attacks and other social engineering tactics.

Regular software updates: Organizations should ensure that all devices and software are kept up to date with the latest security patches and updates to reduce the risk of malware attacks.

Web application security: Organizations should implement secure coding practices and regularly test web applications for vulnerabilities to reduce the risk of session hijacking attacks.

Incident response plan: Organizations should have an incident response plan in place to quickly respond to and contain account hijacking attacks.

Account hijacking is a serious online security threat that can have significant consequences for individuals and organizations. By implementing a multi-layered approach that includes strong authentication, security awareness training, regular software updates, web application securityand an incident response planorganizations can reduce the risk of account hijacking attacks and protect their sensitive data and systems.

C. Methods for Protecting Data and Resources Stored in the Cloud

Cloud computing has become an increasingly popular way for organizations to store and manage their data and resources. However, as more data is stored in the cloud, it's essential to take appropriate measures to protect that data from unauthorized access and theft. In this chapter, we'll explore the various methods for protecting data and resources stored in the cloud.

C.1. Encryption

Encryption is a crucial method of protecting data and resources stored in the cloud. Encryption involves converting data into a code that can only be read by someone who has the key to decode it. This can help prevent unauthorized access to data, even if the data is intercepted or stolen.

There are two types of encryption: symmetric encryption and asymmetric encryption. Symmetric encryption uses the same key for both encryption and decryption, while asymmetric encryption uses different keys for encryption and decryption.

Cloud providers typically offer encryption services for data stored in the cloud. However, users should also consider encrypting their data before uploading it to the cloud. This provides an additional layer of security, as the data will be encrypted both during transmission and while stored in the cloud.

C.2. Access Control

Access control is another important method of protecting data and resources stored in the cloud. Access control involves setting up rules and policies to control who can access specific data and resources. This can help prevent unauthorized access to sensitive information and resources.

Cloud providers typically offer access control features such as user authentication and role-based access control (RBAC). User authentication involves verifying the identity of users before allowing them to access specific data and resources. RBAC involves assigning specific roles to users and providing access to resources based on those roles.

Users should also consider implementing their own access control policies. This can include limiting access to sensitive data and resources to only those who need it and regularly reviewing access controls to ensure they are up to date and effective.

C.3.   Network Security

Network security is another important method of protecting data and resources stored in the cloud. This involves securing the network infrastructure used to transmit data to and from the cloud.

Cloud providers typically offer network security features such as firewalls and virtual private networks (VPNs). Firewalls help prevent unauthorized access to the network, while VPNs encrypt data transmitted over the network.

Users should also consider implementing their own network security measures. This can include using strong passwords and two-factor authentication, monitoring network activity for unusual behaviorand regularly updating network security software.

C.4.   Regular Security Assessments

Regular security assessments are an essential part of maintaining cloud security. These assessments can include vulnerability assessments, penetration testing and security audits. By conducting regular security assessments organizations can identify and remediate vulnerabilities in their cloud environment, helping to prevent security incidents.

C.5.   Backup and Disaster Recovery Planning

Backup and disaster recovery planning is the process of preparing for and responding to potential data losses and system failures in the cloud environment. This includes the creation of backup copies of sensitive data and the development of a disaster recovery plan that outlines the steps to be taken in the event of a security incident. By having a backup and disaster recovery plan in place organizations can help minimize the impact of data loss and system failures in the cloud.

C.6.   Monitoring and Detection

Monitoring and detection are the processes of monitoring the cloud environment for security threats and incidents and detecting when a security incident has occurred. This can include the use of security tools such as firewalls, intrusion detection systems and security information and event management (SIEM) systems. By monitoring and detecting potential security incidents organizations can respond quickly to prevent significant harm and minimize the impact of security incidents.

There are various methods for protecting data and resources stored in the cloud. By implementing a combination of these methods organizations can help prevent unauthorized access to sensitive data and minimize the impact of security incidents. However, it's important to stay informed about the latest security threats and to continuously monitor and assess the security of their cloud environment to ensure the protection of sensitive data and resources.

VI. MOBILE DEVICE SECURITY

A. Overview

As technology continues to advance, more and more people are relying on their mobile devices to stay connected and get things done. From making payments to accessing sensitive information, our smartphones and tablets are an integral part of our daily lives. However, with this increased reliance on mobile devices comes a greater risk of security threats.

Mobile security refers to the measures taken to protect mobile devices and the information stored on them from unauthorized access, theft and other types of attacks. This includes protecting data stored on the device, such as personal information and sensitive documents, as well as protecting the device itself from theft and physical damage.

There are several key reasons why mobile security is becoming increasingly important. First, mobile devices are becoming more powerful and are being used for more sensitive tasks, such as online banking and accessing corporate networks. This means that the stakes are higher if a device is lost, stolen or compromised. Second, mobile devices are more vulnerable to attacks than traditional computers because they often run on less secure operating systems, such as iOS and Android and are more likely to be used in public places where attackers can more easily exploit vulnerabilities.

To ensure the security of your mobile device and the information stored on it, it is important to take a multi-layered approach. This can include implementing strong passwords, using encryption to protect sensitive data and regularly updating your device's operating system and applications. In addition, it is important to be mindful of the risks associated with public Wi-Fi networks and to only download apps from trusted sources.

Mobile security is becoming increasingly important as more people rely on their mobile devices for sensitive tasks. To protect your information and device from threats, it is important to take a multi-layered approach and to be vigilant about potential security risks. In the following chapters, we will dive deeper into the specific types of threats that mobile devices face, as well as the methods for protecting against them.

Before delving into the intricacies of physical security for mobile devices, it's essential to comprehend the various risks that threaten these devices. Physical threats pose one of the most significant risks to the security of mobile devices. These threats include theft, loss, unauthorized access, tamperingand physical damage. Addressing these risks demands a multi-layered approach that encompasses both preventive and reactive measures.

B. Types of Mobile Security Threats and How They Work

Mobile devices have become an integral part of our daily lives, providing us with instant access to information and communication. However, as the use of mobile devices has increased, so have the risks associated with them. In this chapter, we will discuss the various types of mobile security threats and how they work.

B.1. Malware

As we discussed, malware is a type of software that is designed to cause harm to a device. In this section, we will explore the types of mobile security threats, with a particular focus on malwares.

Types of Malwares on Mobile Security

Trojan

Trojans are one of the most common types of malware on mobile devices. These malicious programs are designed to look like legitimate software but contain hidden code that performs unauthorized actions on the device. Once a Trojan has been installed, it can perform a variety of malicious activities, including stealing personal data, installing additional malwareand more.

Ransomware

As we examined before, ransomware is a type of malware that locks the victim's device or encrypts their files, rendering them inaccessible. The attacker then demands a ransom payment in exchange for restoring access to the device or files. Ransomware attacks have become increasingly common on mobile devices in recent years, with attackers using social engineering tactics to trick users into installing the malware.

Adware

Adware is a type of malware that displays unwanted advertisements on the victim's device. These ads can be very intrusive, popping up at random times and interrupting the user's normal activities. Adware is often bundled with legitimate apps, making it difficult for users to detect and remove.

Spyware

Spyware is a type of malware that is designed to secretly monitor the victim's activity on their device. This can include recording keystrokes, tracking location, accessing personal dataand more. Spyware can be difficult to detect and can pose a significant risk to the victim's privacy and security.

How Malwares Work on Mobile Devices?

Malwares on mobile devices can work in a variety of ways, depending on their type and purpose. However, there are some common techniques that are used by many malwares.

Social Engineering

Social engineering is a technique that is commonly used by attackers to trick users into installing malwares on their devices. This can include tactics such as phishing emails, fake app storesand more. Social engineering attacks are designed to exploit the victim's trust or curiosity and encourage them to take actions that put their device and data at risk.

Exploiting Vulnerabilities

Many malwares on mobile devices take advantage of vulnerabilities in the device's operating system or installed apps. These vulnerabilities can be used to gain root access to the device, bypass security measuresand more. Once the malware has gained access to the device, it can carry out its malicious activities without being detected.

B.2.   Malicious Apps

Malicious apps are a common way for attackers to distribute malwares on mobile devices. These apps are designed to look like legitimate apps, but contain hidden code that performs malicious activities. Malicious apps can be distributed through app stores or by tricking users into downloading them from fake websites.

Protecting Against Malwares on Mobile Devices

Protecting against malwares on mobile devices requires a multi-layered approach that includes both technical and non-technical measures.

Technical Measures

Technical measures for protecting against malwares on mobile devices include installing antivirus software, keeping the device's operating system and apps up to dateand using firewalls and other security software. These measures can help detect and prevent malwares from infecting the device.

Non-Technical Measures

Non-technical measures for protecting against malwares on mobile devices include being cautious when installing apps, avoiding clicking on suspicious links or opening attachments in emailsand being aware of social engineering tactics. Users should also regularly back up their data and be prepared to restore their device to a previous state if it becomes infected with malware.

Malwares on mobile devices pose a significant threat to users' privacy and security. These malicious programs can take many forms, from Trojans and ransomware to adware and spyware. To protect against malwares on mobile devices, users should take a multi-layered approach that includes both technical and non-technical measures. By staying informed about the latest threats and taking steps to protect their devices, users can minimize the risk of falling victim to mobile security threats.

B.3.   Phishing

As we discussed before, phishing is a type of social engineering attack that is designed to trick users into revealing sensitive information. This can be done through emails, text messages or phone calls that appear to be from a trusted source but are actually from a malicious attacker. These types of attacks often use fake login pages, fake alerts or fake software updates to trick users into entering their personal information.

Rogue mobile apps

Rogue mobile apps are malicious applications that are disguised as legitimate apps but are actually designed to steal sensitive information. These types of apps can be downloaded from third-party app stores or from unofficial sources and can often contain malware.

Man-in-the-Middle (MitM) attacks

We know that MitM attacks occur when an attacker intercepts and manipulates the communication between two devices. We examined that kind of attack before. This type of attack can be used to steal sensitive information, such as login credentials or to inject malware into a device.

Unsecured Wi-Fi networks

Using unsecured Wi-Fi networks, such as those found in public places, can leave a device vulnerable to attack. This is because unsecured Wi-Fi networks do not have the same level of security as secure networks, making it easier for attackers to intercept communication and steal sensitive information.

There are a variety of different types of mobile security threats, each with their own unique methods of operation. It is important to be aware of these threats and to take steps to protect your mobile devices, such as using a mobile security app, avoiding unsecured Wi-Fi networks and being cautious when downloading apps and opening emails. By taking these precautions, you can help keep your devices and sensitive information safe and secure.

C. Methods for Protecting Mobile Devices and their Data

There are several methods for protecting mobile devices and their data that you can implement to minimize the risk of security incidents.

C.1. Software Updates

Regular software updates can fix known security vulnerabilities in your mobile device's operating system. Keep your device updated to the latest version of the operating system to stay protected against security threats.

C.2. Strong Passwords

A strong password is your first line of defense against unauthorized access to your device. Make sure to use a strong and unique password for your device.

C.3. Device Locks

Device locks are security mechanisms that require users to provide a passcode, PINor password to unlock their mobile devices. The strength of the lock depends on the complexity of the chosen authentication method. Users are encouraged to select strong passcodes that are not easily guessable and avoid using easily identifiable information, such as birthdays or names.

In 2016, researchers conducted a study on smartphone passcodes by analyzing over 3.4 million four-digit PINs. Shockingly, the study found that the most commonly used PIN was "1234," followed closely by "0000." This lack of security awareness among users highlights the importance of promoting the use of strong and unique passcodes.

Biometric Authentication: Biometric authentication uses unique physical or behavioral characteristics of an individual to verify their identity. Common biometric methods used in mobile devices include fingerprint recognition, facial recognition, iris scanningand voice recognition.

Biometric authentication, such as fingerprint or facial recognition, can provide an additional layer of security. However, it's essential to ensure that these biometric data are securely stored and processed to prevent potential misuse.

In 2019, a security researcher successfully bypassed the facial recognition feature on a popular smartphone by using a 3D-printed mask of the owner's face. This case demonstrated the need for manufacturers to continuously improve biometric technologies to prevent such spoofing attempts.

C.4.   Fingerprint Authentication in Banking Apps

Many mobile banking apps have implemented fingerprint authentication to provide secure and convenient access for users. In a study by a cybersecurity firm, it was found that some banking apps stored users' fingerprint data in an insecure manner. This vulnerability raised concerns about the privacy and security of sensitive biometric data, urging app developers to adopt more robust encryption methods.

C.5. Facial Recognition and Law Enforcement

Law enforcement agencies have started using facial recognition technology to identify suspects and find missing persons. While this technology has shown promising results, concerns have been raised about its potential misuse and impact on individual privacy. It is crucial to establish clear guidelines and regulations to ensure the responsible and ethical use of biometric data.

C.6. Two-Factor Authentication

Two-Factor Authentication (2FA) provides an extra layer of security beyond passwords or PINs. By requiring users to provide a second form of authentication, such as a one-time code sent to their mobile device, the risk of unauthorized access is greatly reduced. Organizations should encourage the use of 2FA to enhance security for both personal and business-related mobile devices.

C.7. Mobile Security Apps

A mobile security app can provide added protection to your device by scanning for malware, blocking unwanted calls and texts and backing up your data.

C.8. Be Cautious When Downloading Apps

Only download apps from trusted sources, such as the App Store or Google Play. Read reviews and ratings before installing. Malicious apps can infect your device with malware or steal your personal information. Mobile applications often contain sensitive data and interact with various device features. Therefore, ensuring the security of applications is crucial. Users should avoid sideloading apps from unknown origins to reduce the risk of malware.

C.9. Connect to Secure Wi-Fi Networks

Public Wi-Fi networks are notorious for their lack of security, making them vulnerable to eavesdropping attacks. When connecting to public Wi-Fi, mobile devices may become vulnerable to various cyber threats, such as data interception or man-in-the-middle attacks. To mitigate these risks, many mobile users turn to Virtual Private Networks (VPN) for enhanced security and privacy.

C.10. Public Wi-Fi Risks

Packet Sniffing: On open public Wi-Fi networks, packet sniffing tools can be used to intercept unencrypted data transmitted between the device and the network. This includes sensitive information like login credentials, credit card details and personal messages.

Man-in-the-Middle Attacks (MITM): In a MITM attack, an attacker intercepts and relays communication between the user and the network, potentially altering or stealing data in transit.

Rogue Hotspots: Attackers can set up rogue Wi-Fi hotspots with names similar to legitimate networks to trick users into connecting to them. Once connected, the attacker can capture sensitive information.

C.11. Virtual Private Networks (VPN)

VPNs are security tools that create a secure and encrypted tunnel between the user's device and a VPN server. When connected to a VPN, all internet traffic is routed through this encrypted tunnel, protecting it from interception and ensuring online privacy.

Encryption: VPNs use strong encryption protocols to secure data transmitted over the internet. This ensures that even if intercepted, the data remains unreadable to unauthorized parties.

IP Address Masking: VPNs hide the user's real IP address by assigning them a temporary IP address from the VPN server's location. This helps protect the user's identity and location.

Bypassing Geo-Restrictions: VPNs allow users to access content and services that may be geo-restricted or blocked in their location. By connecting to a VPN server in a different country, users can appear as if they are accessing the internet from that location.

Dangers of Untrustworthy VPNs

While VPNs can enhance security, users should be cautious about using untrustworthy or malicious VPN services:

Data Logging: Some VPN providers may log user activity and data, compromising the user's privacy and defeating the purpose of using a VPN.

Malware and Adware: Free or unverified VPNs may inject ads, track user activityor even distribute malware to the user's device.

Data Leaks: Poorly configured or untrustworthy VPNs may suffer from data leaks, revealing user information despite the supposed encryption.

C.12. Secure Communication Protocols

Mobile devices use secure communication protocols, such as SSL/TLS (Secure Sockets Layer/Transport Layer Security) to encrypt data during transmission. These protocols establish secure connections between the device and servers, ensuring that data exchanges are protected from interception and tampering.

In May 2019, Whatsapp disclosed a severe vulnerability that was exploited by the notorious Pegasus spyware developed by the NSO Group. The vulnerability allowed attackers to inject spyware into targeted devices through a malicious Whatsapp voice call. The spyware could then gain access to the device's data, including messages, callsand other sensitive information, effectively bypassing Whatsapp's end-to-end encryption.

The incident raised concerns about the security of messaging apps even with end-to-end encryption in place. Whatsapp quickly released a patch to address the vulnerability and urged users to update their apps to the latest version to protect themselves from potential attacks.

In 2017, security researchers from the University of California, Berkeley, published a report suggesting that Whatsapp's implementation of Signal Protocol (the encryption protocol used by Whatsapp for end-to-end encryption) may contain a backdoor. The researchers found that Whatsapp servers could potentially alter the encryption keys when a user is offline, which could allow them to intercept and read messages without the users knowledge.

Whatsapp responded to the report, explaining that the behavior was not a backdoor but a design trade-off made to ensure usability and message delivery. They argued that such a design decision was necessary to prevent messages from being lost when a user changes devices or reinstalls Whatsapp. However, the report raised concerns among some security experts, highlighting the need for transparent security practices in messaging apps.

While Whatsapp's end-to-end encryption is generally considered robust and provides a high level of security for user communications, no encryption system is infallible. The case studies above demonstrate that vulnerabilities and weaknesses can be found even in well-designed encryption implementations.

For users, enabling encryption features on their mobile devices is crucial to ensuring the security and privacy of their data. By making encryption a priority, we can create a safer mobile ecosystem that empowers users to enjoy the convenience of mobile devices without compromising their data security.

C.13. Encryption

Data encryption is a fundamental aspect of mobile device security, ensuring that sensitive information stored on the device remains protected from unauthorized access. Encryption involves converting plain text data into ciphertext using cryptographic algorithms, making it unintelligible to anyone without the appropriate decryption key. Mobile devices use various encryption techniques to secure data at rest and data in transit, providing a robust defense against potential threats.

Encryption at Rest

Encryption at rest refers to the encryption of data stored on the mobile device's internal storage or external memory. It prevents unauthorized access to data if the device is lost, stolen or accessed by malicious actors.

In 2018, a survey found that nearly 70 million smartphones were lost or stolen in the United States alone. In such cases, encryption at rest becomes crucial. Encrypted data ensures that even if the physical device falls into the wrong hands, the sensitive information remains inaccessible.

Full Disk Encryption (FDE)

Full Disk Encryption is a common approach used to encrypt all data on the device's storage. When FDE is enabled, the entire storage is encrypted, including the operating system, applicationsand user data. The decryption key is typically derived from the user's passcode, PINor biometric authentication.

Both Android and iOS devices offer built-in support for full disk encryption. On Android, devices running Android 6.0 (Marshmallow) and above have FDE enabled by default. On iOS, all devices since iPhone 3GS and iPad (1st generation) come with hardware encryption, protecting user data using the device's unique identifier (UID) and user passcode.

File-Based Encryption (FBE)

File-Based Encryption is an evolution of FDE, introduced to address the limitations of FDE on devices with multiple users or profiles. With FBE, each user's data is encrypted separatelyand access is controlled by individual user credentials.

Encryption in Transit

Encryption in transit secures data as it travels between the mobile device and external servers or other devices. This is crucial when data is transmitted over networks such as Wi-Fi, cellular data or Bluetooth.

C.14. Remote Wipe

Remote wipe is a security feature that allows users or administrators to erase all data on a mobile device remotely. This capability is especially crucial when a device is lost or stolen, as it prevents unauthorized access to sensitive information, such as emails, contacts, photosand documents.

To enable remote wipe, the device must be connected to the internet. Users can trigger the remote wipe from a web portal or a companion app associated with the device. The command is sent to the device over the internet. Upon receiving the command, the device initiates the wiping process. Depending on the device and its settings, remote wipe may erase all data including user settings and applications, returning the device to its factory default state.

Apple's "Find My iPhone" is a popular example of remote wipe in action. In one instance, a user reported their iPhone stolen and remotely initiated a wipe command using Find My iPhone. The thief turned off the device and attempted to restore it to bypass the remote wipe. However, as soon as the device connected to the internet during the setup process, the remote wipe command took effect, erasing all data and rendering the stolen iPhone useless.

C.15. Tracking

Tracking allows users or administrators to locate a lost or stolen mobile device in real-time. Tracking is enabled through GPS or other location-based services, providing the device's geographical coordinates to help users pinpoint its location on a map.

To enable tracking, the device's location services must be activated and the device must have an active internet connection. Users can track their devices through a web portal or a companion app associated with the device. This feature can help users identify the approximate location of their device, aiding in recovery efforts or notifying law enforcement about the device's whereabouts.

Android devices offer a similar feature called "Find My Device." In one case, a user lost an Android phone and used Find My Device to track its location. The user discovered that the phone was left behind in a public place and was able to retrieve it promptly, thanks to the tracking feature.

While remote wipe and tracking are powerful security tools, they raise privacy and ethical considerations. Users must be cautious about remotely wiping a device with personal data, especially if the device has the potential for recovery or is in the hands of someone who may return it.

Remote wipe and tracking are indispensable features that bolster the security of mobile devices and protect sensitive information. By enabling users to remotely wipe data from lost or stolen devices and track their location, these features empower users to take immediate action to safeguard their data.

C.16. Device Management Solutions

Device Management Solutions (DMS) are comprehensive platforms that allow organizations to centrally manage and control mobile devices used within their network. These solutions provide administrators with the ability to enforce security policies, configure settings, deploy applicationsand monitor devices remotely. DMS offers a unified approach to managing a fleet of mobile devices, ensuring consistent security and compliance across the organization.

DMS enable administrators to enforce security policies on mobile devices. These policies may include password complexity requirements, screen lock timeouts, encryption settingsand restrictions on app installations. Centralized policy enforcement ensures that devices comply with the organization's security standards and reduce the risk of security breaches.

DMS allows organizations to deploy, updateand remove applications on mobile devices efficiently. Administrators can control which applications are allowed or restricted, ensuring that only authorized and vetted apps are installed on company-owned devices. This feature helps prevent the installation of malicious or unapproved apps that could compromise security.

DMS provide real-time monitoring and reporting on the status of mobile devices. Administrators can track device health, battery levels, storage usageand network connectivity. This monitoring capability allows for proactive troubleshooting, identifying potential issues before they become significant problems.

DMS enables administrators to push Over-the-Air updates to mobile devices, including security patches, operating system updates and software upgrades. Keeping devices up to date with the latest software ensures that they are protected against known vulnerabilities and exploits.

In case of device loss or theft, DMS allows administrators to remotely wipe the data on the device, preventing unauthorized access to sensitive information. This feature is especially critical for safeguarding company data when devices are lost or stolen.

Dangers of Device Management Solutions

Privacy Concerns

While DMS offers organizations enhanced security, it also raises privacy concerns, particularly when used in a Bring Your Own Device (BYOD) environment. Employees may feel uncomfortable with their personal devices being monitored or controlled by their employer, leading to potential conflicts and challenges in adopting DMS.

Data Breach Risks

The centralized control provided by DMS can be a double-edged sword. If the DMS platform is compromised, it could provide a single point of entry for attackers to gain access to a large number of mobile devices. Organizations must implement robust security measures for the DMS platform to protect against such risks.

Device Ownership and Employee Privacy

In Bring Your Own Device scenarios, DMS may raise issues related to device ownership and employee privacy. Employees may feel that their personal devices are under excessive control or that their privacy is compromised. Balancing organizational security needs with employee privacy rights is a challenge that requires careful consideration.

Dependency on DMS Availability

Organizations that heavily rely on DMS may face operational disruptions if the DMS platform experiences downtime or technical issues. Over-dependence on DMS may lead to difficulties in managing devices manually during such periods.

Device Management Solutions offer significant benefits for organizations seeking to secure and efficiently manage their mobile devices. By providing centralized control, policy enforcementand remote management capabilities, DMS enhances device security and streamlines device administration.

However organizations must be mindful of the potential privacy and security risks associated with DMS implementation. Striking the right balance between security, privacyand user experience is essential to ensure the successful adoption of DMS and the protection of both organizational data and employee privacy. Robust security measures should be in place to safeguard the DMS platform itself, as compromising it could have severe consequences for the entire device fleet.

C.17.   Physical Security

Physical barriers are essential to preventing unauthorized access to mobile devices. For example, screen protectors with privacy filters can obscure the screen from prying eyes. Additionally, protective cases not only shield devices from physical damage but also limit access to ports and buttons, reducing the risk of tampering. Simple practices, such as not leaving devices unattended in public places, keeping them out of sight in vehicles and storing them securely when not in use can prevent theft and unauthorized access.

C.18. Secure Disposal

When disposing of old or damaged mobile devices, users must ensure that all data is securely wiped from the device. A factory reset is not always sufficient to remove all traces of sensitive information. Using specialized data erasure software or services can guarantee that data is permanently deleted, protecting against potential data breaches.

C.19. Secure Data Backup

Mobile devices are susceptible to loss, damage or theft. Therefore, implementing secure data backup procedures is essential to prevent data loss in such scenarios. Regularly backing up data to secure cloud storage or external devices ensures that critical information remains accessible even if the physical device is compromised.

C.20. Secure Boot

Secure Boot is a process that verifies the authenticity and integrity of each component of the booting process before allowing it to run. It ensures that only trusted and digitally signed bootloaders, operating system kernelsand device drivers are executed during the boot-up sequence. Any attempt to load unsigned or tampered code is prevented, protecting the device from malicious software that may attempt to take control during the early stages of booting.

During Secure Boot, each bootloader and component is checked against cryptographic signatures provided by the device manufacturer or the operating system vendor. If the signatures match and the components pass the integrity checks, the boot process continues. If any component fails verification, the boot process is haltedand the device enters a recovery mode, where it may attempt to restore the device to a known good state or provide the user with options to address the issue.

C.21. Firmware Integrity

Firmware Integrity ensures that the firmware, which is low-level software that controls hardware functionality, remains unaltered and free from unauthorized modifications. Firmware is present in various components of mobile devices, such as the bootloader, radio interfacesand device controllers.

Firmware integrity is maintained by employing cryptographic checksums or digital signatures. During firmware updates, the device verifies the authenticity of the new firmware using these cryptographic mechanisms. If the firmware fails to pass the integrity check, the update process is aborted, preventing the installation of potentially malicious firmware.

In 2015, a severe security vulnerability called "Stagefright" was discovered in the Android operating system. The vulnerability allowed attackers to compromise Android devices by sending a specially crafted multimedia message (MMS). Stagefright could be triggered remotely and potentially affect millions of Android devices.

As a response to this critical security flaw, device manufacturers and Google issued security updates to patch the vulnerability. Secure Boot and Firmware Integrity played a crucial role in the deployment of these updates. Devices with Secure Boot enabled were protected from the installation of malicious software attempting to exploit the Stagefright vulnerability.

Secure Boot and Firmware Integrity heavily rely on regular security updates from the device manufacturer or operating system vendor. These updates include fixes for known vulnerabilities and security patches to keep the device's software up to date and resistant to emerging threats. Regularly updating the device's firmware and operating system is essential to maintain the effectiveness of these security mechanisms.

Secure Boot and Firmware Integrity are essential security features in mobile devices that ensure the device boots up with trustworthy software and prevents unauthorized modifications to the firmware. By verifying the integrity of the boot process and firmware components, these mechanisms protect against boot-level attacks and maintain the overall security of the device. Regular security updates from the manufacturer are crucial to keeping these security features effective against evolving threats and vulnerabilities.

C.22. Physical Storage Media

Many mobile devices support expandable storage through microSD cards or USB drives. Users should be aware of the potential risks associated with these external storage media. Storing sensitive data on removable media should be avoided or if necessary, it should be encrypted to maintain confidentiality.

By following these methods, you can protect your mobile device and its sensitive data from security threats. However, it's important to remember that no single method can provide complete protection, so it's important to use multiple layers of security to keep your device and its data secure.

D. Wi-Fi Security

In this chapter, we will examine the various vulnerabilities and best practices for Wi-Fi security.

Understanding Wi-Fi Networks

Wi-Fi, short for Wireless Fidelity, is a technology that allows devices to connect to a network wirelessly. A typical Wi-Fi network consists of a router or access point that communicates with various devices such as laptops, smartphones and IoT devices. These devices use radio waves to transmit and receive data, making it a convenient and accessible way to stay connected.

Wi-Fi Security Fundamentals

D.1. Encryption Protocols

Encryption protocols play a vital role in securing Wi-Fi networks from malicious attackers. We'll start with an overview of encryption and its significance in the context of Wi-Fi security, then explore various encryption protocols, both historical and modern, to equip you with the knowledge needed to make informed decisions when securing your Wi-Fi networks.

Understanding Encryption

Encryption is the process of converting plain text (data in its original form) into cipher text (encrypted data) using an algorithm and an encryption key. The primary objective of encryption is to protect sensitive information from unauthorized access, ensuring that only authorized parties can decipher and read the data.

Before we examine the specifics of Wi-Fi encryption algorithms, it is essential to understand why encryption is vital for wireless networks. When data is transmitted over the air, it is susceptible to eavesdropping and unauthorized access. Without encryption, attackers can intercept sensitive information, such as passwords, personal data or financial transactions, compromising the privacy and security of users. Encryption ensures that data is scrambled into an unintelligible format during transmission, making it indecipherable to anyone without the proper decryption key.

Encryption protocols rely on two fundamental components:

Algorithms: These are mathematical functions used to perform the actual encryption and decryption of data. The strength and complexity of the encryption algorithm directly impact the security level of the encryption protocol.

Encryption Keys: Encryption keys are used in combination with algorithms to encrypt and decrypt data. There are two main types of keys: symmetric and asymmetric. Symmetric encryption uses the same key for both encryption and decryption, while asymmetric encryption uses a pair of keys - a public key for encryption and a private key for decryption.

Historical Encryption Protocols

Wired Equivalent Privacy (WEP)

WEP was one of the earliest encryption protocols used to secure Wi-Fi networks. Unfortunately, it suffered from significant vulnerabilities, making it easily breakable by attackers. WEP's key scheduling algorithm was flawed and the use of a static key made it susceptible to brute-force attacks. As a result, WEP was rapidly replaced by more secure protocols.

Wi-Fi Protected Access (WPA)

WPA was introduced as an interim solution to address the weaknesses of WEP. It used the Temporal Key Integrity Protocol (TKIP) to provide improved security. However, it still had its vulnerabilities, primarily due to the reliance on legacy WEP for compatibility purposes.

In the early days of Wi-Fi, WEP was the standard security protocol. However, it soon became evident that WEP's encryption algorithm was easily crackable, leaving wireless networks vulnerable to unauthorized access and data breaches. As cyber threats continued to escalate, the Wi-Fi Alliance (a non-profit organization responsible for promoting and certifying Wi-Fi technology) recognized the urgency for a stronger security solution.

In response to these concerns, the Wi-Fi Alliance introduced Wi-Fi Protected Access (WPA) in 2003. Initially, WPA was considered an intermediate solution while the more robust Wi-Fi Protected Access 2 (WPA2) was under development. WPA2 eventually succeeded WPA and became the most widely adopted security protocol for wireless networks. However, WPA still remains relevant and is often used in older devices and legacy systems.

WPA significantly improved the security of wireless networks by implementing key advancements over WEP. The primary encryption method used in WPA is Temporal Key Integrity Protocol (TKIP), which dynamically changes encryption keys during data transmission, making it much harder for attackers to crack the key. Additionally, WPA employs a Message Integrity Check (MIC) to ensure that data packets have not been tampered with during transmission.

Another crucial security feature introduced in WPA is the use of the Extensible Authentication Protocol (EAP) framework, allowing for more secure authentication methods such as 802.1x, which uses a RADIUS (Remote Authentication Dial-In User Service) server for central authentication and authorization.

WPA2

WPA2, based on the Advanced Encryption Standard (AES), became the industry standard for Wi-Fi security. AES, a symmetric encryption algorithm, brought significant improvements in both security and performance. WPA2's implementation of AES-CCMP (Counter Mode with Cipher Block Chaining Message Authentication Code Protocol) delivered robust encryption, significantly reducing the risk of attacks.

One of the critical elements of WPA2's security is the four-way handshake, a process that allows a client to securely connect to an access point. During this handshake, both the client and access point establish the encryption keys used for data transmission. Understanding the intricacies of the four-way handshake is essential for comprehending the logic behind the Wi-Fi encryption process fully.

- Authentication Request: The client initiates the connection by sending an authentication request to the access point.

- Authentication Response: In response, the access point sends an authentication response, indicating that it is ready to proceed with the handshake.

- Key Generation: Once the authentication is confirmed, the client and the access point engage in a process of key generation. This process involves exchanging nonces (random numbers) and other cryptographic elements to create a shared encryption key without transmitting the actual key over the air.

- Group Key Handshake: Lastly, a group key handshake occurs, allowing the client and access point to establish the key used for broadcast and multicast communication within the network.

Modern Encryption Protocols

WPA3

In response to emerging threats and the need for higher security standards, WPA3 was introduced. WPA3 implements

Simultaneous Authentication of Equals (SAE), also known as Dragonfly, which strengthens the authentication process and provides forward secrecy. It mitigates offline dictionary attacks and improves the security of devices with limited user interfaces.

Opportunistic Wireless Encryption (OWE)

OWE, also known as "Enhanced Open," is designed to provide encryption even on open Wi-Fi networks without requiring users to enter passwords. It helps protect users from passive eavesdropping and man-in-the-middle attacks, enhancing security without compromising user experience.

Selecting the Right Encryption Protocol

Choosing the appropriate encryption protocol depends on various factors, including the network's sensitivity, compatibility with existing devices and security requirements. Consider the following when making your decision:

Security: Always prioritize protocols with stronger encryption and fewer vulnerabilities.

Compatibility: Ensure that the selected protocol is supported by all devices on the network.

Regulations: In some cases, specific regulations or standards may mandate the use of certain encryption protocols.

Best Practices for Implementation

Regardless of the encryption protocol chosen, some best practices apply:

Regular Updates: Keep the firmware and software of networking equipment up-to-date to patch potential vulnerabilities.

Strong Passwords: Use strong and unique passwords for Wi-Fi access, ensuring resistance against brute-force attacks.

Guest Networks: Set up guest networks to segregate guest users from the main network and protect sensitive data.

Understanding the importance of encryption in Wi-Fi security is crucial in safeguarding data from malicious actors. Remember to choose the right encryption protocol based on your specific needs and implement best practices to maintain a robust and secure Wi-Fi network.

D.2.   SSID Broadcasting

The Service Set Identifier (SSID) is the name of your Wi-Fi network. While it may seem convenient to broadcast the SSID, hiding it can add an extra layer of security. However, this measure alone won't keep determined attackers at bay. So it should be used in conjunction with other security practices.

D.3.   Securing Your Wi-Fi Network

Strong Passwords

A robust password is the first line of defense against unauthorized access to your Wi-Fi network. Avoid using common passwords and include a mix of uppercase and lowercase letters, numbers and special characters. Longer passwords are generally more secure, so aim for a minimum of 12 characters.

Regularly Update Router Firmware

Manufacturers release firmware updates to address security vulnerabilities and enhance performance. Make it a habit to check for and apply firmware updates regularly to keep your router secure.

Disable Remote Management

Unless you require remote access for specific reasons, disable remote management on your router. This reduces the risk of unauthorized individuals attempting to access and control your router settings.

MAC Address Filtering

Media Access Control (MAC) address filtering allows you to specify which devices can connect to your network based on their unique hardware MAC addresses. While it's not foolproof, combining this with other security measures can help reinforce your network's defenses.

Guest Networks

Many modern routers offer a guest network feature, allowing you to create a separate network for visitors. This isolates their devices from your main network, preventing potential unauthorized access to your private files and devices.

Wi-Fi Protected Setup (WPS)

Disable WPS if your router supports it. WPS can be vulnerable to brute-force attacks, allowing attackers to gain access to your network by guessing the PIN.

D.4.   Fake Wi-Fi Networks

Fake Wi-Fi networks, also known as rogue Wi-Fi networks or evil twin Wi-Fi networks are a growing cybersecurity concern. These deceptive networks have been used by hackers to exploit the trust of unsuspecting users, making them a powerful tool in conducting criminal activities.

Creation of the Fake Network

Setting up a fake Wi-Fi network is surprisingly straightforward for skilled attackers. They can utilize off-the-shelf wireless routers or even specially crafted hardware to create these rogue networks. By customizing the network's Service Set Identifier (SSID) to match that of a well known and trusted public

Wi-Fi hotspot, the attacker deceives users into believing they are connecting to a legitimate network. This is the main logic of fake Wi-Fi networks.

To make the fake network more enticing, attackers might use common names such as "Free Wi-Fi" or "Guest Wi-Fi" which are commonly found in public spaces where people expect to find open Wi-Fi connections. The goal is to trick users into connecting to their malicious network instead of the genuine one.

Deceptive Authentication

Users are often accustomed to connecting automatically to known networks or those with stronger signals. Attackers exploit this behavior by configuring their fake Wi-Fi network to have a more potent signal than nearby legitimate networks. As a result, the user's device may automatically connect to the rogue network without their knowledge.

Moreover, some attackers use more advanced techniques such as deauthentication attacks, also known as deauth attack. In a Wi-Fi network, devices like smartphones or laptops connect to an access point (router) using a four-way handshake process. During this process, access point and device exchange cryptographic keys to establish a secure connection. An attacker can use specialized software or tools to generate and transmit deauthentication packets over the Wi-Fi network. These packets impersonate the access point and target the connected devices. When the targeted device receive the deauthentication packets, interpret them as a legitimate disconnection request from the access point and disconnect from network. After being deauthenticated, the device attempt to reconnect to the Wi-Fi network. Depending on the network and the device settings, they may automatically reconnect or require manual reconnection by the user.

Deauth attack is essentially a denial-of-service (DoS) attack to the users of a Wi-Fi network. Disrupting their ability to use the network for a brief period. These attacks can be particularly effective in crowded areas with numerous Wi-Fi devices.

It's important to note that deauthentication attacks usually require the attacker to be physically close to the Wi-Fi network because Wi-Fi signals have limited range.

Common way to defend against deauthentication attacks is to implement proper Wi-Fi security measures such as using strong encryption protocols like WPA2 or WPA3, keeping Wi-Fi equipment firmware up to date and monitoring the network for suspicious activities.

Targeted Attacks

Fake Wi-Fi networks are not only deployed in public places but can also be specifically set up to target particular individuals or organizations. Attackers might employ these networks near corporate offices or government buildings to gain unauthorized access to sensitive information.

Protecting Yourself from Fake Wi-Fi Networks

Verify Wi-Fi Networks: Always verify the correct name and credentials of the Wi-Fi network with the venue or staff before connecting.

Use VPN: VPNs create a secure tunnel between your device and a server, ensuring that even if the data is intercepted, it remains encrypted and unreadable to attackers.

Avoid Unsecured Websites: Ensure you only visit websites using HTTPS encryption, especially when entering sensitive information like passwords or credit card details. Look for the padlock symbol and "https://" in the URL, indicating a secure connection.

Forget Unfamiliar Networks: After using a public Wi-Fi network, forget or remove the network from your device's saved networks to prevent automatic connections in the future.

Update Your Devices: Keeping your devices and apps up to date with the latest security patches is essential to mitigate potential vulnerabilities that attackers could exploit.

Use a Firewall: Configure your device's firewall to restrict unauthorized access and communication between your device and other networks.

Monitor Battery Drain: Fake Wi-Fi networks can drain your device's battery faster than usual due to the increased activity. If you notice unusually fast battery depletion, be cautious about the Wi-Fi network you are connected to.

Public Wi-Fi Awareness: Be cautious when connecting to public Wi-Fi networks, especially those that do not require passwords or have suspiciously strong signals.

Cybercriminals can spy on your online activity, steal your personal information or infect your device with malware. To protect yourself and your data, here are some useful tips for public Wi-Fi awareness:

VII. ENDPOINT SECURITY

A. Overview

Endpoint security refers to the protection of devices such as computers, smartphones and other online devices from cyber threats. These devices are often the first line of defense for a network and it is essential to secure them to ensure the overall security of an organization's network.

Why Endpoint Security is Important?

Endpoints are the weakest link in an organization's security chain and securing them is essential for protecting sensitive information and data. These devices often have access to sensitive data, such as financial information, personal identification or confidential business information and are vulnerable to attacks. If an attacker gains access to an endpoint, they can easily spread malware and steal sensitive data, compromising the entire network.

With the rise of remote work and the proliferation of mobile devices, the traditional network perimeter has essentially disappeared. This shift makes endpoint security all the more important. Endpoint security solutions provide a centralized approach to protect all endpoints connected to a network.

Components of Endpoint Security

Endpoint security typically involves several components working together. These may include Antivirus/Anti-Malware Softwares, Firewalls, Intrusion Prevention Systems, Sandboxing, Encryption, Email Security and Data Loss Prevention.

Implementing Endpoint Security

Implementing endpoint security involves deploying security solutions on all endpoints, configuring settings according to best practices, regularly updating and patching these solutions and continuously monitoring endpoint status.

Endpoint security faces several challenges, including:

Increasingly Sophisticated Threats: Cyber threats are becoming more advanced and harder to detect. Attackers are constantly developing new methods to bypass traditional security measures.

Growing Number of Endpoints: With the rise of remote work and Bring Your Own Device (BYOD) policies, the number of endpoints that need to be secured has significantly increased. This makes it more difficult for IT teams to manage and secure these devices.

Lack of Visibility: It can be challenging for organizations to gain full visibility into all their endpoints, especially with the use of personal devices and IoT devices in the network.

Patch Management: Keeping all endpoints updated with the latest patches is a daunting task, especially for large organizations with numerous devices.

User Behavior: End-users often engage in risky behavior such as clicking on malicious links or using weak passwords, which can compromise endpoint security.

The Role of AI in Endpoint Security

Artificial Intelligence (AI) is playing an increasingly important role in endpoint security. AI can analyze vast amounts of data to identify patterns and anomalies that may indicate a threat. This allows for faster detection and response times, even for previously unknown threats.

The Future of Endpoint Security

The future of endpoint security lies in integrated solutions that not only offer traditional protection but also incorporate newer technologies like artificial intelligence and machine learning. These technologies can help in proactive threat hunting and behavior analysis to identify and mitigate threats before they can cause significant damage.

Emerging trends in endpoint security include:

Human-Centric Security Design: It's a transformative approach to cybersecurity that places the individual, rather than technology, threat or location at the center of control design and implementation. This approach acknowledges that humans are both the weakest link and the first line of defense in cybersecurity. By addressing human behavior and considering the user in every aspect of security design, businesses can reduce the likelihood of human error and strengthen their overall cybersecurity posture.

Cloud Migration: The most significant trend in the endpoint security market is the acceleration of organizations migrating to the cloud. The cloud is driving new endpoint security strategies. Enterprises are interested in transitioning to cloud-delivered security to reduce cost/complexity, simplify security for mobile users and adopt new capabilities. However, the fact that "the concept of cloud is ultimately someone else's computer", should never be ignored.

B. Types of endpoint security threats and how they work

B.1.   Malware

Malware refers to any software designed to cause harm to a computer system or steal sensitive information. Some of the most common types of malware include viruses, worms, Trojans and ransomware. These malicious programs can be delivered to a device through email attachments, downloads from untrusted websites or via malicious software updates.

B.2.   Phishing

Phishing is a type of attack that uses social engineering tactics to trick users into revealing sensitive information. The attacker will often create a fake email or website that looks like a legitimate source and ask the user to provide sensitive information, such as login credentials or financial information.

B.3.   Man-in-the-Middle Attacks

This type of attack occurs when an attacker intercepts and alters the communication between two parties. The attacker can modify or steal sensitive information during the transmission.

B.4.   Drive-by Downloads

Drive-by downloads occur when a user visits a website that contains malicious code. The code is automatically executed on the device, potentially installing malware or stealing sensitive information.

There are a number of ways that malicious code can be embedded in a website. One common way is through the use of exploit kits. Exploit kits are malicious software that can exploit vulnerabilities in web browsers and other software. When a user visits a website that contains an exploit kit, the kit can exploit a vulnerability in the user's software and download malware onto the device.

Another way that malicious code can be embedded in a website is through the use of social engineering techniques. Social engineering techniques are used to trick users into clicking on malicious links or opening malicious attachments. For example, an attacker might send an email that appears to be from a legitimate source, such as a bank or credit card company. The email might contain a malicious link. When clicked, it will download malware onto the user's device.

Drive-by downloads can be a serious threat to computer security. Malware that is installed through a drive-by download can steal personal information such as passwords and credit card numbers. It can also damage or destroy files or even take control of the infected device.

Users should be careful about what links they click on, what attachments they open and only visit websites that they trust to protect themselves from drive-by downloads.

B.5.   Rootkits

Rootkits are a type of malware that are designed to hide their presence on a compromised system. They do this by modifying or replacing system files, processesand data structures, in order to create a covert channel for communication between the attacker and the compromised system. Rootkits can also alter the behavior of other applications and operating system components, in order to hide their own malicious activities.

Rootkits typically gain access to a system by exploiting a vulnerability or by tricking a user into running a malicious program. Once installed, a rootkit can perform a variety of malicious activities, including stealing data, monitoring user activityand allowing attackers to control the compromised system remotely.

Types of Rootkits

There are several types of rootkits, each with their own unique characteristics and methods of operation. Some common types of rootkits include:

User-level Rootkits: These rootkits operate at the user-level, meaning that they require the user to have administrative privileges on the compromised system in order to function. They typically modify system files and processes to hide their presence and allow attackers to maintain persistent access to the system.

Kernel-level Rootkits: These rootkits operate at the kernel-level, meaning that they have complete access to the operating system and can modify its behavior in a variety of ways. They are more difficult to detect and remove than user-level rootkitsand can be used to create backdoors, steal dataand perform other malicious activities.

Bootloader Rootkits: These rootkits infect the system's bootloader, which is responsible for loading the operating system into memory. By modifying the bootloader, a rootkit can load itself into memory before the operating system, making it virtually undetectable.

Hypervisor Rootkits: These rootkits operate at the hypervisor level, which is a layer of software that sits between the operating system and the hardware. By modifying the hypervisor, a rootkit can intercept and modify system calls, allowing it to remain hidden from the operating system and other security measures.

Detecting and Removing Rootkits

Detecting and removing rootkits can be a difficult and time-consuming process as they are designed to evade detection and removal. Some common techniques for detecting and removing rootkits include:

Scanning for suspicious files and processes: Antivirus software and other security tools can scan a system for suspicious files and processes that may be associated with a rootkit.

Checking system logs: Rootkits can often be detected by examining system logs for unusual activity or signs of tampering.

Performing a clean installation of the operating system: In some cases, the only way to completely remove a rootkit is to perform a clean installation of the operating system, wiping the hard drive and reinstalling all software and data.

Using specialized rootkit removal tools: There are several specialized tools available for detecting and removing rootkits.

These are just a few examples of the types of threats that can impact endpoint devices. It is essential to be aware of the various types of threats and understand how they work to effectively protect against them.

B.6.   Botnets

Botnets are one of the most common and dangerous threats on the internet. They are networks of compromised devices that are controlled by hackers to perform various malicious activities such as spamming, stealing data, launching distributed denial-of-service (DDoS) attacks and more.

What is a botnet?

A botnet is a group of devices that have been infected by malware and are remotely controlled by a hacker, also known as a botmaster or a bot herder. The devices can be computers, smartphones, routers or any other online device. The infected devices are called bots or zombies and they usually do not show any signs of infection to the users.

A botnet can consist of hundreds, thousands or more bots, depending on how many devices the hacker can infect and control. The hacker can use the botnet to perform various tasks that require a large amount of computing power or bandwidth such as:

-    Sending spam emails or messages to millions of recipients
-    Stealing personal or financial information from the infected devices or their networks

- Launching DDoS attacks that overwhelm the target website or server with a huge amount of traffic
- Distributing malware or ransomware to other devices
- Mining cryptocurrencies using the processing power of the infected devices
- Conducting click fraud or ad fraud by generating fake clicks or impressions on online advertisements

How does a botnet work?

A botnet works by following these steps:

The hacker creates or obtains a malware program that can infect and control devices. The malware program may be a trojan, worm, virus or any other type of malware. The hacker distributes the malware program to potential victims using various methods such as phishing emails, malicious downloads, drive-by downloads, exploit kits or social engineering. The malware program infects the devices and establishes a connection with a server or a peer-to-peer network. The server or the P2P network is used by the hacker to send commands and updates to the bots and receive information from them. The hacker uses the botnet to perform the desired tasks by sending commands to the bots. The bots execute the commands and report back to the hacker.

Different types of botnets

Botnets can be classified into different types based on their architecture, communication method or purpose. Some of the common types of botnets are:

Centralized botnets: These botnets use a command and control server or a group of servers to communicate with the bots. The hacker can easily control and update the bots using the server but the server is also a single point of failure that can be detected and taken down.

Decentralized botnets: These botnets use a P2P network to communicate with the bots. The bots can communicate with each other without relying on a central server, making them more resilient and difficult to disrupt. However P2P botnets may also have some drawbacks such as higher bandwidth consumption and lower scalability.

Hybrid botnets: These botnets combine both centralized and decentralized architectures to achieve a balance between efficiency and resilience. For example, some hybrid botnets use a server for initial infection and updates but switch to a P2P network when it comes to command execution and data transmission.

Mobile botnets: These botnets target mobile devices such as smartphones and tablets. Mobile botnets can exploit the vulnerabilities in mobile operating systems, applications or networks to infect and control the devices. Mobile botnets can also use SMS messages or mobile data connections to communicate with the bots.

IoT botnets: These botnets target internet-of-things (IoT) devices such as routers, cameras or smart TVs. IoT botnets can take advantage of the weak security measures and default passwords of many IoT devices to infect and control them. IoT botnets can generate massive amounts of traffic for DDoS attacks due to the large number of devices involved.

How to prevent botnet attacks?

Botnet attacks can cause serious damage to individuals, businesses and organizations. Therefore, it is important to take preventive measures to protect your devices from being infected and used by hackers. Some of the best practices for preventing botnet attacks are:

Keep your software up to date: New viruses and malware are created every day, so it is important to update your operating system, applications, antivirus software and firewall regularly to fix any security vulnerabilities and protect your device from new threats.

Avoid suspicious links and attachments: Do not click on links or open attachments from unknown or untrusted sources. They may contain malware that can infect your device. Also, do not download software from unverified websites or peer-to-peer networks. They may also contain malware or unwanted programs.

Install a botnet prevention tool: Use a botnet prevention tool that can monitor your network traffic and detect any signs of botnet activity. It can also block any malicious connections or commands from the hacker and alert you of any potential threats.

C. Methods for Protecting Endpoints from Attacks

Endpoints are the entry points for cyberattacks, making them one of the most vulnerable parts of any network. These can be laptops, desktops, servers, mobile devices and even Internet of Things (IoT) devices. To protect endpoints from cyberattacks, there are several methods that can be used.

C.1. Antivirus and Anti-malware software

Installing antivirus and anti-malware software on all endpoints is the first line of defense against cyberattacks. These software programs detect and remove viruses, malware, spyware and other malicious software that can compromise endpoint security.

C.2. Firewall

A firewall acts as a barrier between the endpoint and the Internet, protecting the endpoint from unauthorized access. Firewalls can also be configured to block incoming and outgoing traffic based on specific rules and policies.

C.3.   Software Updates

Regularly updating all software on the endpoint, including the operating system, browsers and other applications, is important to keep the endpoint secure. Software updates often include security patches that address known vulnerabilities.

C.4.   Network Segmentation

Segmenting the network into smaller parts helps to limit the impact of a security breach. Endpoints can be assigned to different security zones and policies can be implemented to limit the access between zones.

C.5.   Encryption

Encrypting sensitive data stored on endpoints makes it difficult for attackers to access or steal the data, even if the endpoint is compromised.

C.6.   Backup and Recovery

Regularly backing up important data and having a disaster recovery plan in place is critical for quickly recovering from a security breach.

C.7.   Endpoint Detection and Response (EDR) tools:

Endpoint Detection and Response (EDR): EDR tools continuously monitor and collect data from endpoints to detect threats, trigger alerts and initiate response actions. They provide visibility into endpoint data and use advanced analytics to identify potential threats that may have bypassed initial defenses.

C.8.   Network Access Control (NAC): NAC solutions control access to the network based on a device's compliance with a defined security policy. This includes factors like the presence of antivirus software, up-to-date patches and specific configurations. Non-compliant devices can be restricted or blocked from accessing the network.

C.9.   Mobile Device Management (MDM): With the prevalence of smartphones and tablets in the workplace, Mobile Device Management (MDM) has become a key part of endpoint security. MDM tools allow IT teams to manage and secure these devices, enforcing policies, managing apps and protecting against threats.

VIII. IDENTITY AND ACCESS MANAGEMENT (IAM)

A. Overview

IAM is a critical component of any organization's security infrastructure, responsible for ensuring that the right people have access to the right resources at the right time. In this chapter, we'll provide an overview of what IAM is and why it's important, so you can better understand how it fits into the overall picture of internet security.

What is Identity and Access Management?

IAM refers to the policies, processes and technologies that organizations use to manage and secure digital identities and the access they have to sensitive data and systems. This includes everything from creating and managing user accounts and passwords to controlling who can access what resources and when.

Why IAM is Important?

IAM is important because it helps organizations ensure that their sensitive data and systems are protected from unauthorized access and theft. By controlling who has access to what resources organizations can reduce the risk of breaches, protect their data from theft and maintain the privacy and security of their customers and employees.

IAM also helps organizations comply with various regulations and standards, such as the General Data Protection Regulation (GDPR) and the Payment Card Industry Data Security Standard (PCI DSS), which require organizations to implement strict security measures to protect personal data and sensitive information.

Overall, IAM is an essential part of any organization's security strategy, providing a foundation for protecting sensitive data and systems, maintaining the privacy and security of individuals and ensuring compliance with relevant regulations and standards.

In the next pages, we'll examine the different components of IAM and explore the various techniques and technologies that organizations can use to protect their digital identities and access to sensitive data and systems.

B. Types of IAM Threats and How They Work

Identity and Access Management (IAM) is an essential component of an organization's security strategy. The primary aim of IAM is to ensure that only authorized individuals have access to sensitive data and systems within the organization. However, just like any other security measure, IAM is also susceptible to various threats that can compromise its effectiveness. In this chapter, we will look at the different types of IAM threats and how they work.

B.1.   Social Engineering Attacks

These attacks exploit human psychology rather than technical vulnerabilities, making them particularly challenging to prevent. In the context of IAM, social engineering attacks aim to deceive individuals into revealing their credentials or granting unauthorized access to sensitive systems. Attackers often pose as trusted entities such as colleagues or IT support staff to gain the victim's trust and manipulate them into divulging confidential information.

There are several common techniques used in social engineering attacks:

Phishing: This is perhaps the most well-known form of social engineering. In a phishing attack, the attacker sends an email or message that appears to come from a trusted source, such as a bank or a colleague. The message typically contains a link to a fake website where the victim is prompted to enter their credentials.

Baiting: Baiting involves offering something enticing to the victim in exchange for their information. For example, an attacker might leave a USB drive loaded with malware in a public place, hoping that someone will find it and plug it into their computer.

Pretexting: In pretexting attacks, the attacker creates a fabricated scenario (the pretext) to engage the victim. The attacker might pretend to need certain information from the victim to confirm their identity.

These techniques can be highly effective because they exploit human tendencies to trust others and desire for convenience. We'll deeply examine social engineering and its dangers in the next chapters.

B.2.   Password Attacks

Despite the rise of multi-factor authentication, passwords remain a primary method of authentication, making them a prime target for attackers. In the context of IAM, password attacks aim to crack or bypass passwords to gain unauthorized access to systems.

There are several techniques that attackers use:

Brute Force Attacks: This is a trial-and-error method used to obtain information such as a user password or personal identification number (PIN). In a brute force attack, automated software is used to generate a large number of consecutive guesses to the value of the desired data.

Dictionary Attacks: Unlike brute force attacks that try all possible combinations, dictionary attacks try a prearranged list of values such as words in a dictionary. Attackers often use dictionaries of commonly used passwords, which can be surprisingly effective given the number of people who use simple, easy-to-guess passwords.

Password Spraying: This technique involves trying a small number of commonly used passwords against a large number of accounts. This method can be effective and stealthy because it makes only a few attempts on each account, reducing the likelihood of triggering account lockouts or other security defenses.

Keylogger Attacks: A keylogger is a type of surveillance technology used to monitor and record each keystroke typed on a specific computer's keyboard. Attackers use keyloggers to capture confidential user data like usernames, passwords, credit card numbers, etc.

Rainbow Table Attacks: A rainbow table is a precomputed table for reversing cryptographic hash functions, usually for cracking password hashes. Attackers use rainbow tables to speed up the password cracking process.

Credential Reuse Attacks: Many users tend to use the same password across multiple platforms. Attackers exploit this habit by trying the same set of username and password obtained from one breach in other platforms.

Shoulder Surfing: This is a simple and non-technical kind of attack where the attacker directly observes the user's screen or keyboard to get their password. It often happens in crowded places and requires direct observation skills.

Phishing via Software: Some attackers trick users into installing malicious software that appears to be legitimate. Once installed, this software may display fake login screens to capture the user's credentials.

These attacks highlight the importance of strong password policies within an organization. Encouraging users to create complex, unique passwords and implementing account lockout policies after a certain number of failed login attempts can help mitigate the risk of password attacks. Additionally, using multi-factor authentication can add an extra layer of security by requiring users to provide more than one form of identification.

B.3.   Insider Threats

Insider threats pose a significant risk to an organization's Identity and Access Management (IAM) systems. These threats originate from individuals within the organization who have authorized access to sensitive systems and data. They can be employees, contractors or partners who misuse their access rights, either intentionally or unintentionally, to cause harm to the organization.

Insider threats can take various forms:

Unauthorized Access: This occurs when insiders use their legitimate access rights to access sensitive information that they do not need for their job functions. This could be driven by curiosity, malicious intent or even coercion by external parties.

Theft of Confidential Information: Insiders may steal confidential information for personal gain or to benefit a third party. This could involve copying sensitive data onto portable storage devices or sending it via email or other means to external parties.

Deliberate Sabotage: In some cases, disgruntled employees may deliberately sabotage critical systems, causing disruptions to business operations and potentially leading to significant financial and reputational damage.

Accidental Actions: Not all insider threats are malicious. Sometimes, well-meaning employees may accidentally cause security incidents. For example, they might fall victim to phishing attacks, use weak passwords or fail to follow security best practices.

Mitigating insider threats requires a combination of technical controls and administrative measures. Regular audits of access rights can help ensure that employees only have access to the resources they need for their job functions. Security awareness training can help employees understand the risks and follow best practices. Additionally, implementing advanced security solutions like User Behavior Analytics (UBA) can help detect unusual behavior that may indicate an insider threat.

B.4.   Man-in-the-Middle Attacks

In the context of Identity and Access Management (IAM), MitM attacks can be used to steal user credentials or intercept sensitive information as it is being transmitted between systems.

In a typical MitM attack, the attacker positions themselves in the communication network, often by exploiting vulnerabilities in the network infrastructure or by using social engineering techniques to trick users into connecting to malicious networks. Once in position, the attacker can monitor all data being transmitted between the two parties, capturing sensitive information such as usernames, passwords, credit card numbers and other personal data.

MitM attacks can take several forms. One common type is a Wi-Fi eavesdropping attack, where the attacker sets up a rogue Wi-Fi network and tricks users into connecting to it. Once connected, all data transmitted over the network can be captured by the attacker.

Another type of MitM attack is a DNS spoofing attack. In this case, the attacker manipulates the Domain Name System (DNS) entries to redirect traffic to a malicious server under their control. The user believes they are communicating with a legitimate server, but all their data is being sent to and captured by the attacker.

MitM attacks can be particularly dangerous because they can be difficult to detect. The communication appears normal to both parties involved and there may be no obvious signs of an attack. This makes these attacks a significant threat to both individuals and organizations.

Preventing MitM attacks requires a combination of strong security practices. This includes using secure communication protocols such as HTTPS and SSL/TLS, regularly updating and patching systems to fix security vulnerabilities, educating users about the risks of unsecured networks and phishing attacks and implementing robust network security measures such as firewalls and intrusion detection systems.

B.5.   Session Hijacking

Session hijacking, also known as session sidejacking, cookie hijacking or session key hijacking is a type of security attack where an attacker intercepts and takes control of a user's session. This is often achieved by obtaining the user's session ID or exploiting vulnerabilities in the authentication process.

Once the attacker has control of a user's session, they can masquerade as the user and perform actions on their behalf. This could include accessing sensitive data, modifying data or even performing transactions. The severity of the impact depends on the privileges of the hijacked user account - if it's an account with administrative privileges, the consequences could be disastrous.

There are several methods that attackers use to perform session hijacking:

Session Sniffing: In this method, attackers use a packet sniffer to intercept network traffic between the user's computer and the web server. If the communication isn't encrypted, the attacker can easily capture the session ID.

Cross-Site Scripting (XSS): Attackers use XSS vulnerabilities in web applications to inject malicious scripts into web pages viewed by users. These scripts can then steal session cookies.

Session Replay: In this method, attackers intercept and save the network traffic (containing session information). They can then replay this traffic to impersonate the user.

Man-in-the-Browser attack: This is a more advanced form of session hijacking where malware running on the user's computer intercepts and alters communication between the browser and the web server, even if it's encrypted.

Preventing session hijacking involves several measures such as encryption of the data in transit, regular regeneration of session IDs, validating user requests and implementing secure coding practices to prevent XSS attacks.

B.6.   Credential Stuffing

Credential stuffing is a type of cyber attack where attackers use lists of stolen credentials, obtained from previous data breaches, to try to gain unauthorized access to various online accounts. This method is particularly effective due to the common practice of password reuse across multiple platforms.

In the context of Identity and Access Management (IAM), credential stuffing attacks pose a significant threat as they can be used to compromise user accounts, gain unauthorized access to sensitive data or escalate privileges within an organization.

The process of credential stuffing typically involves three stages:

Data Breach: The attacker obtains a list of usernames and passwords from a data breach. These breaches can involve millions of user credentials and are often available for purchase on the dark web.

Testing: The attacker uses automated scripts or bots to test the stolen credentials against multiple websites or services. This is often done at a large scale and can involve thousands of login attempts per minute.

Account Takeover: If the login attempt is successful, the attacker gains access to the account. They can then carry out malicious activities such as stealing sensitive information, making fraudulent purchases or spreading malware.

To protect against credential stuffing attacks organizations can implement several security measures:

Multi-Factor Authentication (MFA): MFA requires users to provide two or more verification factors to gain access to a resource such as an application, online account or a VPN. This makes it more difficult for attackers to gain access to accounts, even if they have the correct username and password.

Account Lockouts: After a certain number of failed login attempts, the account is locked out, preventing further attempts. This can slow down or stop automated login attempts.

Password Complexity and Diversity: Encouraging users to create complex and unique passwords for each account can reduce the success rate of credential stuffing attacks.

Regularly Monitor and Audit Accounts: Regular monitoring of accounts can help detect unusual activity that may indicate a credential stuffing attack.

B.7   Privilege Escalation

Privilege escalation is a critical aspect of cybersecurity, where a user gains access rights beyond those initially assigned. It's a significant threat in the realm of Identity and Access Management (IAM) as it can lead to unauthorized access to sensitive data and systems.

There are two types of privilege escalation: vertical and horizontal.

Vertical Privilege Escalation (also known as privilege elevation) occurs when a user with lower privileges accesses functions or content reserved for higher-privileged accounts. This type of escalation is often the result of system vulnerabilities or misconfigurations. For instance, an application might unintentionally allow a standard user to execute administrative commands or a system administrator might mistakenly assign excessive permissions to a user account.

Horizontal Privilege Escalation happens when a user accesses resources granted to a peer user. This type of escalation typically involves users with similar privilege levels. For example, one employee might gain access to another employee's personal data or email account.

To mitigate the risk of privilege escalation organizations should adopt the principle of least privilege (PoLP). This principle involves providing users with the minimum levels of access necessary to complete their tasks. Regular audits of user privileges can also help identify and correct instances of excessive access rights.

Organizations also should invest in robust IAM solutions that include features like multi-factor authentication which can prevent unauthorized users from escalating privileges even if they have obtained a user's credentials.

Continuous monitoring and immediate response to suspicious activities can help detect and prevent privilege escalation attacks. Security Information and Event Management (SIEM) systems can be particularly effective in this regard as they aggregate log data from various sources and use advanced analytics to identify potential security incidents.

C. Methods for Controlling Access to Resources and Sensitive Data

As we have learned in the previous chapter, IAM is a critical component of internet security. In this chapter, we'll discuss the methods that organizations use to control access to resources and sensitive data.

To begin, let's start with the basics. Controlling access to resources and sensitive data involves setting up policies and procedures that dictate who can access what and when. This can involve creating user accounts and setting up permissions, as well as implementing technical controls such as firewalls, intrusion detection systems and encryption. The goal is to ensure that only authorized users can access sensitive data and resources and that access is granted only when it is needed and for legitimate purposes.

C.1. Password

One of the most common methods for controlling access to resources and sensitive data is through the use of passwords. Passwords are a simple and effective way to control access, as long as they are properly managed. This means using strong passwords, requiring users to change them frequently and storing them securely.

C.2.   Multi-Factor Authentication (MFA).

MFA adds an extra layer of security by requiring users to provide two or more forms of identification in order to access resources and sensitive data. This could involve a password combined with a security token, a smart card or a biometric identifier such as a fingerprint or facial recognition. MFA helps prevent unauthorized access by making it much more difficult for hackers to impersonate authorized users.

C.3.   Role-Based Access Control (RBAC)

Another method of controlling access to resources and sensitive data is through the use of role-based access control. RBAC involves creating roles for different groups of users and then assigning specific permissions to each role. For example, a role for administrators might have full access to sensitive data, while a role for end users might only have read-only access. This helps ensure that access is properly controlled and that sensitive data is protected.

It is important to regularly monitor and audit access to resources and sensitive data. This can involve reviewing logs, running reports and performing penetration testing to identify potential vulnerabilities. This helps organizations stay on top of changes to their security environment and quickly address any potential threats.

IX. CRYPTOGRAPHY

A. Overview

Diving deep in cryptography is never enough to understand completely as it's actually a bottomless ocean. Its depths are filled with complex algorithms and protocols that provide the foundation for secure communication. Diving deep into this ocean, one can uncover layers of intricate mechanisms designed to protect data from unauthorized access and manipulation.

The importance of cryptography in cybersecurity cannot be overstated. It serves as the first line of defense in securing sensitive information, ensuring that data remains confidential and integral while in transit or at rest. Cryptography provides the tools necessary to authenticate users, verify the integrity of data and ensure non-repudiation, making it an indispensable part of any robust cybersecurity strategy.

Cryptography encompasses a wide range of techniques, each with its own strengths and weaknesses. Symmetric encryption, for instance, is fast and efficient but requires secure key exchange. Asymmetric encryption solves the key exchange problem but is computationally expensive. Hash functions provide data integrity but are not suitable for encryption. Understanding these nuances is crucial for implementing effective cryptographic solutions.

Moreover, cryptography is a dynamic field that evolves in response to new threats and technological advancements. New cryptographic algorithms are continually being developed to counter emerging threats, while older ones become obsolete. Staying abreast of these changes is essential for maintaining effective cybersecurity defenses.

However, despite its complexity and ever-changing nature, cryptography is not an unsurpassable challenge. With a solid understanding of its fundamental principles and a willingness to continually learn and adapt, one can navigate this bottomless ocean effectively.

A.1.　Cryptography Basics

Cryptography, the art of writing or solving codes, is a fundamental pillar of cybersecurity. It's a complex field with a rich history and a wide array of techniques but understanding the basics can provide a solid foundation for further exploration. Here are some key concepts:

Encryption and Decryption: Encryption is the process of converting plaintext into ciphertext, a form that is unreadable without the decryption key. Decryption is the reverse process, converting ciphertext back into plaintext.

Symmetric and Asymmetric Encryption: Symmetric encryption uses the same key for encryption and decryption. It's fast and efficient, but key exchange can be a challenge. Asymmetric encryption uses different keys for encryption and decryption (public and private keys). It's more secure but also more computationally intensive.

Hash Functions: A hash function takes an input and returns a fixed-size string of bytes. The output (hash) is unique to each unique input. It's used for verifying data integrity.

Digital Signatures: A digital signature is a cryptographic technique used to verify the authenticity and integrity of a message or document. It provides proof that the message came from the stated sender (authentication) and that it hasn't been tampered with (integrity).

Key Exchange Protocols: Key exchange protocols like Diffie-Hellman or RSA allow two parties to establish a shared secret key over an insecure channel. This key can then be used for symmetric encryption.

Public Key Infrastructure (PKI): PKI is a set of roles, policies, hardware, software and procedures needed to create, manage, distribute, use, store and revoke digital certificates and manage public-key encryption.

Cryptography can be divided into two broad categories: symmetric cryptography and asymmetric cryptography. Each has its unique strengths and applications in securing digital information.

Symmetric Cryptography

Symmetric cryptography, also known as secret key cryptography, involves the use of a single key for both encryption (converting readable data into an unreadable format) and decryption (converting the unreadable data back into its original format). The same key is shared between the sender and the receiver. This method is fast and efficient, making it ideal for encrypting large amounts of data. However, the challenge lies in securely exchanging the key between parties without it being intercepted.

Examples of symmetric cryptography algorithms include Advanced Encryption Standard (AES), Data Encryption Standard (DES) and Triple DES (3DES).

Asymmetric Cryptography

Asymmetric cryptography, also known as public key cryptography, uses two different keys: a public key for encryption and a private key for decryption. The public key is freely distributed while the private key is kept secret by the owner. This eliminates the problem of secure key exchange that is present in symmetric cryptography. However, asymmetric cryptography requires more computational resources, making it slower than symmetric cryptography.

Examples of asymmetric cryptography algorithms include RSA (Rivest-Shamir-Adleman), Diffie-Hellman and Elliptic Curve Cryptography (ECC).

Both symmetric and asymmetric cryptography play vital roles in securing digital information.

A.2.   Cryptographic Algorithms

As we examined before, cryptographic algorithms are mathematical formulas and processes used to encode and decode information. Some of the most commonly used cryptographic algorithms include Advanced Encryption Standard (AES), Rivest-Shamir-Adleman (RSA), Digital Signature Algorithm (DSA) and Elliptic Curve Cryptography (ECC).

Each cryptographic algorithm has its own strengths and weaknesses and it is important to choose the right algorithm for the specific task. For example, AES is fast and secure, making it well suited for encrypting large amounts of data while RSA is slow but more secure, making it well suited for digital signatures.

A.3.   Cryptographic Protocols

Cryptographic protocols are sets of rules and procedures used to securely communicate and exchange information. They ensure that the information is securely encrypted and transmitted even in the presence of attackers trying to intercept or modify the information. They also verify that the information is from the intended source and has not been tampered with during transmission.

There are several cryptography protocols that are widely used in cybersecurity:

Secure Sockets Layer (SSL) and Transport Layer Security (TLS): . They are commonly used to secure web communication and protect sensitive data, such as credit card numbers, passwords and personal information. SSL/TLS provide confidentiality, data integrity and authenticity, making them essential for secure communication over the internet.

Internet Protocol Security (IPSec): This protocol suite secures Internet Protocol (IP) communications by authenticating and encrypting each IP packet in a data stream.

Secure Shell (SSH): This cryptographic network protocol enables secure remote login from one computer to another over an insecure network.

Pretty Good Privacy (PGP): This program provides cryptographic privacy and authentication for data communication, often used for signing, encrypting and decrypting texts, emails, files, directories and whole disk partitions.

Hyper Text Transfer Protocol Secure (HTTPS): This is an extension of HTTP used for secure communication over a computer network, widely used on the Internet.

Kerberos: Named after the three-headed dog from Greek mythology, Kerberos is a network authentication protocol designed to provide strong authentication for client/server applications. It works on the basis of 'tickets' which serve as a means to verify the identities of clients for various services.

Secure/Multipurpose Internet Mail Extensions (S/MIME): S/MIME is a widely accepted protocol for sending digitally signed and/or encrypted mail. It ensures the confidentiality and integrity of the email messages.

Secure File Transfer Protocol (SFTP): SFTP is a network protocol that provides file access, file transfer and file management functionalities over any reliable data stream. It ensures that the data is securely transferred using a private and safe data stream.

RADIUS (Remote Authentication Dial-In User Service): RADIUS is a networking protocol that provides centralized Authentication, Authorization and Accounting (AAA) management for users who connect and use a network service.

Lightweight Directory Access Protocol (LDAP): LDAP is an open, vendor-neutral, industry standard application protocol for accessing and maintaining distributed directory information services over an Internet Protocol (IP) network.

OpenVPN: OpenVPN is an open-source software application that implements virtual private network (VPN) techniques for creating secure point-to-point or site-to-site connections in routed or bridged configurations and remote access facilities. Kerberos: Named after the three-headed dog from Greek mythology, Kerberos is a network authentication protocol designed to provide strong authentication for client/server applications. It works on the basis of 'tickets' which serve as a means to verify the identities of clients for various services.

WireGuard: WireGuard is a free and open-source software application and communication protocol that implements virtual private network (VPN) techniques to create secure point-to-point connections in routed or bridged configurations.

Zigbee Security Layers: Zigbee is a specification for a suite of high-level communication protocols used to create personal area networks built from small, low-power digital radios. Zigbee uses 128-bit symmetric encryption keys for its security layers.

Extensible Authentication Protocol (EAP): EAP is an authentication framework frequently used in wireless networks and Point-to-Point connections. It provides a common framework for various methods of authentication.

Message Queuing Telemetry Transport (MQTT): MQTT is a lightweight messaging protocol for small sensors and mobile devices, optimized for high-latency or unreliable networks. It ensures the secure transmission of messages through TLS/SSL protocols.

Real-time Transport Protocol (RTP): RTP is a network protocol for delivering audio and video over IP networks. Secure Real-time Transport Protocol (SRTP) is an RTP profile intended to provide encryption, message authentication and integrity and replay attack protection to the RTP data.

Time-based One-Time Password (TOTP): TOTP is an algorithm that computes a one-time password from a shared secret key and the current time. It's been adopted as Internet Engineering Task Force (IETF) standard and is widely used for two-factor authentication.

B. Methods for Using Cryptography to Secure Communication and Protect Data

Cryptography is a critical component of modern security systems, as it provides a way to protect sensitive information as it travels through networks, is stored on devices and is transmitted between systems. But with the vast array of cryptographic algorithms and protocols available, how do you determine which one is best suited for your needs?

In this chapter, we'll explore the various methods for using cryptography to secure communication and protect data. We'll look at encryption, hashing, digital signatures and certificate authorities. We'll also explore the benefits and limitations of each method, so that you can make an informed decision about which one is right for your organization.

B.1. Encryption

Encryption is a process that uses a mathematical algorithm to convert plaintext data into ciphertext or unreadable code. Encryption is used to protect sensitive data from unauthorized access or theft. It can be used to secure data in transit, such as when sending an email or to secure data at rest, such as when storing data on a device or in the cloud.

There are two main types of encryption: symmetric and asymmetric. Symmetric encryption uses the same key for both encryption and decryption. This means that both the sender and the recipient must have access to the same key in order to communicate securely. Asymmetric encryption, also known as public key cryptography, uses two different keys: a public key and a private key. The public key is used to encrypt the data, while the private key is used to decrypt it. This allows for secure communication between two parties who do not have to share a key.

B.2.   Hashing

Hashing is a one-way process that converts data into a fixed-length string of characters. It's commonly used to secure passwords, as well as to verify the integrity of data. Hashing is a fast and efficient way to compare two pieces of data, as the hash values of two identical pieces of data will always be the same.

B.3.   Digital Signatures

Digital signatures are a way to verify the authenticity and integrity of data. They work by using a combination of encryption and hashing to create a unique signature that is attached to a message. The recipient of the message can then use the sender's public key to verify the signature and ensure that the data has not been altered in transit.

B.4.   Certificate Authorities

Certificate Authorities (CA) are organizations that issue digital certificates, which are used to verify the identity of a website or device. Digital certificates contain information about the website or device, such as its domain name, IP address and the public key used for encryption. When you visit a website with a digital certificate, your browser can verify the identity of the website and ensure that the data transmitted between you and the website is secure.

Cryptography provides a variety of methods for securing communication and protecting data. Whether you choose encryption, hashing, digital signatures or certificate authorities, it's important to understand the strengths and limitations of each method and to choose the one that is best suited for your organization's needs. By using cryptography in combination with other security measures such as firewalls, antivirus software and intrusion detection systems, you can create a comprehensive security system that protects your sensitive data from unauthorized access and theft.

C. Case Studies and Examples of Cryptography in Action

Cryptography is a fascinating field that has been used for centuries to secure communication and protect sensitive information. Today, cryptography plays a critical role in protecting data and maintaining privacy in many different scenarios, including online transactions, cloud storage and wireless communication. In this chapter, we will look at some real-world examples of cryptography in action and see how it is being used to safeguard information and secure communication.

C.1.   SSL/TLS Encryption for Online Transactions

The most common use of cryptography is in online transactions. When you visit a website and see the padlock icon and "https" in the URL, it means that the site is using SSL/TLS encryption to secure your communication. This encryption is used to protect sensitive information, such as passwords and credit card numbers, from being intercepted by attackers. In this way, cryptography is essential for maintaining the security of online transactions and ensuring that sensitive information is kept safe.

C.2.   Encrypted Cloud Storage

Cloud storage is becoming increasingly popular as more and more people store their data in the cloud. To protect this data, encryption is used to encrypt files and data stored on cloud servers. In this way, even if an attacker gains access to the cloud servers, they will not be able to access the encrypted data.

C.3.   Wireless Communication Security

Wireless communication, such as Wi-Fi and Bluetooth, is increasingly used to connect devices and transfer data. To protect this data, encryption is used to secure wireless communication and prevent attackers from intercepting sensitive information. For example, the WPA2 protocol uses AES encryption to protect Wi-Fi networks from unauthorized access.

C.4.   Cryptographic Signatures for Digital Signatures

Cryptographic signatures are used to verify the authenticity of digital documents and electronic transactions. This is accomplished by using a public key infrastructure (PKI), which allows users to verify the authenticity of a signature and ensure that the data has not been tampered with. For example, a digital signature can be used to sign an electronic contract or agreement, making it legally binding.

C.5.   Encrypted Email

Email is one of the most widely used forms of communication and is often used to send sensitive information. To protect this information, encryption can be used to encrypt email messages, making it much more difficult for attackers to intercept the information and read the message. For example, the popular email service provider ProtonMail uses end-to-end encryption to protect the privacy of its users.

These are just a few examples of the many ways that cryptography is used to protect data and secure communication. By understanding these real-world examples, you can see how cryptography is essential for maintaining the security and privacy of sensitive information in today's digital world.

X. INCIDENT RESPONSE AND MANAGEMENT

A. Overview

An incident is any event that disrupts the normal operations of an organization, threatens its security or compromises its data. Incident response is the process of identifying, containing, analyzing and resolving incidents in a timely and effective manner. Incident management is the set of activities that coordinate and oversee the incident response process, such as planning, communication, documentation and improvement.

The main objectives of incident response and management are to minimize the impact of incidents on the organization, restore normal operations as soon as possible, prevent or reduce the likelihood of recurrence and learn from the experience to improve security posture and readiness.

The following sections will cover the main topics related to incident response and management in cybersecurity:

Incident Response Lifecycle: This section will describe the four phases of the incident response lifecycle: preparation, detection and analysis, containment and eradication and recovery and post-incident activity. It will also discuss the best practices, tools and techniques for each phase, such as incident response policies and procedures, threat intelligence sources, digital forensics methods, malware analysis tools, incident reporting formats and lessons learned reports.

Incident Management Frameworks: This section will compare and contrast the different frameworks and standards for incident management, such as NIST SP 800-61, ISO/IEC 27035, ITIL and COBIT. It will also explain how to align the incident management process with the organization's goals, governance, risk management, compliance and business continuity requirements.

Incident Response Team: This section will define the roles and responsibilities of the incident response team members, such as incident manager, incident coordinator, incident handler, technical specialist, legal advisor, public relations officer and senior management. It will also discuss how to recruit, train, equip and evaluate the incident response team members, as well as how to manage their workload, stress and morale during an incident.

Incident Response Challenges: This section will identify the common challenges and pitfalls that may arise during incident response and management, such as lack of resources, skills or authority; conflicting priorities or interests; communication breakdowns; legal or regulatory issues; or insider threats. It will also suggest some strategies and solutions to overcome these challenges and improve the incident response and management process.

B. Steps in the Incident Response Process

The incident response process is a systematic and structured approach to handle and resolve security incidents in an organization. It consists of several steps that aim to identify, contain, analyze and eradicate the incident, as well as recover from its impact and prevent its recurrence. The following sections will cover the main steps in the incident response process and their sub-steps:

B.1.   Preparation

The preparation step involves the following sub-steps:

Developing and updating incident response policies and procedures: The organization should have a clear and comprehensive set of policies and procedures that define the scope, objectives, roles, responsibilities and activities of the incident response process. These policies and procedures should be aligned with the organization's goals, governance, risk management, compliance and business continuity requirements. They should also be reviewed and updated regularly to reflect the changes in the organization's IT environment, threat landscape and best practices.

Defining roles and responsibilities: The organization should establish a dedicated incident response team that consists of qualified and experienced members who can perform various tasks during an incident, such as incident manager, incident coordinator, incident handler, technical specialist, legal advisor, public relations officer and senior management. The roles and responsibilities of each team member should be clearly defined and communicated, as well as their authority, accountability and escalation procedures.

Establishing communication channels: The organization should have effective and secure communication channels that can facilitate the information sharing and coordination among the incident response team members, as well as other stakeholders, such as internal departments, external partners, vendors, customers, law enforcement agencies, media outlets and regulators. The communication channels should include both formal and informal methods, such as phone calls, emails, instant messages, meetings, reports, alerts, notifications and bulletins.

Acquiring and maintaining tools and resources: The organization should have adequate and appropriate tools and resources that can support the incident response process, such as hardware, software, network devices, storage devices, backup systems, forensic tools, malware analysis tools, threat intelligence sources, encryption tools, authentication tools, access control tools and incident response kits. The tools and resources should be tested and verified regularly to ensure their functionality and compatibility.

Conducting training and awareness programs: The organization should conduct regular training and awareness programs for the incident response team members and other employees to enhance their knowledge, skills and capabilities in handling security incidents. The training and awareness programs should cover topics such as incident response policies and procedures, roles and responsibilities, communication channels, tools and resources, threat scenarios, best practices, lessons learned, security awareness, security hygiene, security culture and security behavior.

B.2.   Detection and Analysis

It involves identifying early signs of a security incident, analyzing these signs to differentiate actual threats from false alarms and documenting the incident with all relevant facts and response procedures.

Log Analysis: Examining system logs, network traffic logs and other relevant logs to identify suspicious activities or anomalies.

Intrusion Detection Systems (IDS): Deploying IDS tools to monitor network traffic and identify potential security breaches.

Malware Analysis: Analyzing malware samples to understand their behavior, identify their origin and develop countermeasures.

Threat Intelligence: Leveraging threat intelligence feeds and platforms to stay updated on the latest threats and vulnerabilities.

Digital Forensics: Collecting and analyzing digital evidence to reconstruct events leading up to an incident.

B.3.   Containment and Eradication

It's a critical phase in the incident response process. It focuses on limiting the impact of a security incident and removing any threats from the affected systems. It takes several steps to contain and eradicate the incident.

Quarantine: Isolate the affected systems or networks to prevent further spread of the incident. This may involve disconnecting compromised devices from the network or creating network segmentation to contain the incident.

Investigation: Conduct a thorough investigation to identify the cause, scope and impact of the incident. This includes analyzing logs, examining system configurations and reviewing any available evidence.

Malware Removal: Remove any malicious software or code that was introduced during the incident. This may involve using antivirus tools, manual removal techniques or restoring affected systems from clean backups.

Patch Vulnerabilities: Identify and address any vulnerabilities or weaknesses that were exploited during the incident. Apply necessary patches, updates or configuration changes to prevent similar incidents in the future.

System Hardening: Strengthen the security posture of the affected systems by implementing additional security controls, such as access restrictions, intrusion detection systems or enhanced monitoring.

B.4.   Recovery and Post-Incident Activity

It focuses on restoring normal operations, learning from the incident and improving future incident response capabilities.

System Restoration: Restore affected systems to their pre-incident state by reinstalling software, applying patches or recovering from clean backups.

Data Recovery: Recover any lost or corrupted data caused by the incident. This may involve using data backup solutions or specialized recovery tools.

Security Assessment: Conduct a comprehensive security assessment to identify vulnerabilities exposed during the incident. This includes reviewing system configurations, access controls and security policies.

Lessons Learned: Analyze the incident to identify areas for improvement in incident response procedures, security controls or employee training. Document these lessons learned to enhance future incident response capabilities.

Communication and Reporting: Inform stakeholders about the incident, its impact and the steps taken for recovery. This includes internal communication with employees, management and external communication with customers, partners or regulatory bodies.

Post-Incident Analysis: Perform a thorough analysis of the incident response process to evaluate its effectiveness. Identify any gaps or shortcomings and propose remedial actions to enhance future incident response capabilities.

It is essential to document all activities performed during the steps. This documentation helps organizations maintain an accurate record of the incident and track progress.

C. Methods for Planning and Preparing for Security Incidents

Incident response and management is a crucial aspect of maintaining the security and confidentiality of sensitive information and systems. Preparing for security incidents involves creating a comprehensive incident response plan and conducting regular drills to ensure that the plan is effective. In this chapter, we will explore various methods for planning and preparing for security incidents.

C.1. Developing a Comprehensive Incident Response Plan

A comprehensive incident response plan is an essential part of preparing for security incidents. It outlines the steps that should be taken in the event of a security breach and helps ensure that the response is organized and effective. The plan should be reviewed and updated regularly to reflect changes in the security environment and ensure that it remains relevant.

Key components of an incident response plan include:

- Identification of potential security incidents and the triggers that initiate the incident response process.
- Assignment of roles and responsibilities to different team members to ensure that everyone knows what they should be doing in the event of an incident.

- A clear and concise process for reporting and responding to incidents, including communication protocols and escalation procedures.
- Information on the tools and resources needed to respond to incidents, such as forensics tools and data backup systems.
- Guidelines for post-incident analysis, documentation and reporting.

C.2.   Conducting Regular Drills and Tests

These exercises provide an opportunity to test the effectiveness of the plan, identify areas for improvement and ensure that all team members are familiar with their roles and responsibilities during an incident. Here are some detailed steps to consider:

Establish a Schedule: Determine how often drills should be conducted. This could range from monthly to annually, depending on the nature of your organization and the sensitivity of the data you handle. Regularity is key to ensure that your team is always prepared.

Define Scenarios: Create realistic scenarios based on potential threats your organization might face. These could include phishing attacks, ransomware, data breaches or insider threats. Each scenario should be unique to provide a comprehensive testing environment.

Involve All Relevant Parties: Ensure that everyone who has a role in the incident response plan participates in the drill. This includes IT staff, management and even non-technical staff who may be involved in the response.

Conduct the Drill: Execute the drill according to the defined scenario. Encourage team members to act as they would in a real incident. This might involve isolating systems, analyzing logs or communicating with stakeholders.

Monitor and Record Actions: Have an observer monitor the drill to record actions and responses. This person should note what went well and what didn't and whether team members followed the incident response plan accurately.

Review and Improve: After the drill, hold a debriefing session where you review the observer's notes and discuss improvements that can be made to the plan. Update your incident response plan accordingly.

C.3.   Implementing Access Control Measures

These measures help to prevent unauthorized access to sensitive data and systems, thereby reducing the risk of security incidents.

Identify Resources: Start by identifying the resources that need protection. This could include databases, servers, applications and even physical assets like laptops and mobile devices.

Define User Roles: Create user roles based on job functions. Each role should have the minimum level of access required to perform its associated tasks. This principle, known as the Principle of Least Privilege (PoLP), helps to limit the potential damage from a security breach.

Implement Authentication Mechanisms: Use strong authentication mechanisms to verify the identity of users before granting access. This could include passwords, biometric data or multi-factor authentication.

Deploy Access Control Systems: Implement an access control system that enforces your policies. This could be a simple system like Access Control Lists (ACLs) or a more complex system like Role-Based Access Control (RBAC) or Attribute-Based Access Control (ABAC).

Regularly Review and Update Access Controls: Regularly review your access controls to ensure they are still appropriate for each user role. Update these controls as necessary, especially when employees change roles or leave the organization.

Audit and Monitor Access: Regularly audit and monitor access to your resources. Look for any unusual or suspicious activity that could indicate a security incident.

C.4. Reviewing and Updating Security Policies and Procedures

It's an important aspect of preparing for security incidents. This helps to ensure that the policies and procedures remain relevant and effective and that they reflect changes in the security environment. Security policies and procedures should be reviewed regularly and updated to reflect changes in technology and threats and to ensure that they remain effective.

Preparing for security incidents is a crucial aspect of maintaining the security and confidentiality of sensitive information and systems. A comprehensive incident response plan, regular drills and tests and implementing access control measures and regularly reviewing security policies and procedures can help organizations be better prepared for security incidents. By following these methods organizations can reduce the risk of security incidents and ensure that their response to such incidents is organized, effective and efficient.

D. Vulnerability Assessment

Vulnerability assessment is a process that helps organizations identify and prioritize security risks in their IT systems and applications. It can help prevent cyberattacks, data breaches and compliance violations by finding and fixing security weaknesses before they are exploited by malicious actors. Vulnerability assessment can also improve the overall security posture and performance of an organization by enhancing its awareness, visibility and control over its IT assets.

There are different types of vulnerability assessment, depending on the scope, target and method of the evaluation. Some common types are network-based, host-based, wireless network, application and database assessment. Each type has its own advantages and limitations and may require different tools and techniques to perform effectively.

The vulnerability assessment process typically consists of four steps: identification, analysis, assessment and remediation. In the identification step, the organization scans its IT environment for potential vulnerabilities using automated or manual methods. In the analysis step, the organization verifies and investigates the identified vulnerabilities to determine their root causes and impacts. In the assessment step, the organization ranks and prioritizes the vulnerabilities based on their severity, likelihood and business impact. In the remediation step, the organization implements appropriate solutions or mitigations to eliminate or reduce the vulnerabilities.

Vulnerability assessment is an essential part of a proactive and comprehensive cybersecurity strategy. It can help organizations protect their data, systems and reputation from cyber threats, as well as comply with relevant laws and regulations. However, vulnerability assessment is not a one-time activity, but a continuous process that requires regular updates, reviews and improvements to keep up with the evolving threat landscape.

XII. UNDERSTANDING SOCIAL ENGINEERING

A. Overview

Social engineering is an age old technique that predates the digital era. It manipulates human emotions, behaviors and cognitive biases to trick individuals into revealing sensitive information, granting unauthorized access or performing certain actions that can compromise security. The success of social engineering attacks heavily relies on the ability to deceive and exploit the trust people place in others.

B. Types of Social Engineering Threats and How They Work

B.1.   The Psychology Behind Social Engineering

Trust and Authority

People naturally tend to trust and obey those they perceive as authority figures or legitimate representatives of a company or organization. Attackers exploit this tendency by impersonating authority figures, such as IT personnel, supervisors or executives to gain access to sensitive information or systems. They use confidence and persuasion to convince victims that they have a legitimate reason for their requests.

Reciprocity

The principle of reciprocity influences individuals to feel obligated to return a favor or act kindly when someone does the same for them. Social engineers may initiate a small act of kindness, such as providing a small gift or compliment, to create a sense of indebtedness, encouraging victims to reciprocate with information or access. This technique often plays on the natural inclination of people to be helpful and cooperative.

Fear and Urgency

Social engineers exploit fear and urgency to create panic, making victims act impulsively without thinking rationally. By posing as a threat or conveying a sense of urgency, attackers aim to push individuals into revealing critical data or performing actions they would not otherwise do. Fear of losing access to an account, facing disciplinary action or experiencing a data breach can lead to hasty decision-making.

Curiosity and Greed

Exploiting human curiosity or the desire for financial gain can lead individuals to click on malicious links, open infected attachments or disclose sensitive information. Social engineers often craft enticing messages or offers that appeal to individuals' curiosity about a shocking event or promise of financial gain. These techniques capitalize on the desire for novelty or personal benefit, encouraging victims to take actions without due caution.

B.2.   Psychological Approaches for Cybercriminals

Pretexting and Empathy

Cybercriminals skilled in social engineering often adopt a pretexting approach, where they create a fabricated scenario that appeals to the emotions and empathy of their targets. They use empathy as a tool to build trust with their victims and create a strong emotional connection, making them more likely to divulge sensitive information or perform requested actions.

Rapport Building

Building rapport is a crucial aspect of social engineering. Cybercriminals invest time and effort in understanding their targets' interests, hobbies and personal lives. By creating a sense of familiarity and friendship, attackers gain victims' trust more easily. This approach is commonly employed in spear-phishing attacks, where attackers customize their messages based on publicly available information about the target.

Mirroring and Body Language

In face-to-face interactions, cybercriminals may use mirroring techniques to subconsciously build rapport with their targets. They subtly mimic the target's body language, gestures and speech patterns to create a sense of familiarity and comfort. This mirroring technique helps to establish a deeper level of trust and influence the target's decision-making.

Social Proof and Likability

Cybercriminals often use social proof to manipulate their targets. By showcasing testimonials, references or endorsements from other individuals, they create the illusion of legitimacy and credibility. Similarly, attackers may aim to be likable and pleasant, making it easier for victims to comply with their requests due to the positive impression they create.

B.3.   Common Social Engineering Techniques:

Phishing

Phishing is a prevalent social engineering tactic where attackers send fraudulent emails, messages or websites that imitate legitimate sources, enticing recipients to provide login credentials, financial data or other sensitive information. Phishing attacks can range from basic and easily detectable to sophisticated and highly targeted spear-phishing campaigns. Attackers often use email spoofing and domain impersonation to deceive recipients effectively.

Pretexting

In pretexting, attackers fabricate a plausible scenario to elicit information from victims, such as impersonating coworkers, vendors or authorities. They create a pretext that requires assistance from the victim, leading them to divulge sensitive details or grant unauthorized access. Pretexting requires a good understanding of the organization's structure, personnel and protocols to craft a convincing narrative.

Baiting

Baiting involves enticing victims with offers or freebies such as infected USB drives labeled as important documents or software to trick them into compromising their systems. When unsuspecting victims take the bait and plug in the infected device or run the malware, the malware gains access to the system. Baiting exploits human curiosity and the desire for something valuable without any apparent cost.

Quid Pro Quo

Attackers use quid pro quo to promise something of value in exchange for information or actions. For instance, they might call random employees, posing as technical support and offer free software upgrades, assistance with a supposed technical issue or discounts in return for login credentials or other sensitive information. The lure of receiving something valuable in exchange encourages victims to provide the requested information.

B.4.   Reverse Social Engineering

In reverse social engineering, attackers manipulate victims into believing they need help, gaining their trust to extract sensitive information. They may pose as tech support, claiming to assist with a technical issue, only to extract login credentials or sensitive data from the victim. Reverse social engineering requires a thorough understanding of the victim's needs and concerns.

Real-World Examples

CEO Fraud

A common variant of social engineering involves impersonating high-ranking executives to trick employees into transferring funds to fraudulent accounts. The attacker leverages authority and urgency to pressure employees into making the transfer without proper verification. These attacks can lead to significant financial losses for organizations.

Watering Hole Attacks

A watering hole attack is a type of targeted cyber attack where attackers compromise a website frequented by a specific group of potential victims.

This type of attack typically involves the following steps:

Target Identification: Attackers identify individuals or organizations within a specific target group. This group often shares common characteristics like belonging to a particular industry, geographic location or having a specific area of interest.

Selection of the Watering Hole: Attackers target a website that the chosen group regularly visits or trusts. This could be a forum, blog or news site related to the industry or interest.

Injection of Malicious Code: Attackers inject malicious code into the chosen watering hole website. This code grants the attackers access to the victim's computer when executed.

Waiting Game: The attackers now wait for visitors to the watering hole website. When members of the target group visit the site, they may inadvertently acquire the malicious code.

Compromising the Targets: Once the malicious code infects the computers, the attackers gain access. With this access, they can reach sensitive data.

This type of attack is often more sophisticated and focused compared to general attacks. The target group is usually limited to a specific industry organization or individuals. Therefore, while not a prevalent form of attack, watering hole attacks are employed to hit targets more effectively. Consequently organizations should take this type of attack into consideration when implementing security measures.

B.5.   Defending Against Social Engineering:

Mitigating social engineering threats requires a combination of technical defenses and a security-aware culture:

Security Awareness Training: Regular and engaging security awareness training educates employees about social engineering techniques, promoting a vigilant and informed workforce. Training should cover the latest social engineering tactics, real-world case studies and the psychological tricks employed by cybercriminals to manipulate targets. By understanding how social engineering works and the psychological principles at play, employees can better identify and resist social engineering attempts.

User Behavior Analytics: Implementing user behavior analytics can help organizations detect anomalies and suspicious activities in real-time. UBA systems analyze user activities and behavior patterns to identify deviations from the norm. By detecting unusual login times, access attempts or data access patterns, UBA can provide early warning signs of potential social engineering attacks.

Machine Learning and AI: Leverage machine learning and artificial intelligence to analyze data and identify patterns indicative of social engineering attempts. AI-powered systems can continuously learn from historical data, adapt to emerging threats and improve their accuracy in detecting and preventing social engineering attacks.

Endpoint Protection: Deploy robust endpoint protection solutions that include anti-malware, intrusion detection and data loss prevention features. Endpoint security can help detect and block phishing emails, malicious attachments and other social engineering-related threats before they can compromise user systems.

Continuous Testing and Evaluation: Regularly assess the organization's susceptibility to social engineering attacks through penetration testing and red team exercises. External penetration testers or ethical hackers can simulate social engineering attacks to identify weaknesses in security measures and provide actionable insights to improve defenses.

Strong Password Policies: Enforce strong password policies, including mandatory regular password changes and the use of complex passwords or passphrases. Encourage employees to use password managers to generate and store unique and strong passwords for each account, reducing the risk of successful social engineering attacks based on password guesswork.

Privileged Access Management (PAM): Implement privileged access management solutions to tightly control access to critical systems and data. PAM restricts administrative privileges and employs just-in-time access, ensuring that individuals have access only when necessary and for a limited duration, preventing unauthorized access through social engineering techniques.

Zero Trust Architecture: Adopt a zero trust security approach that requires verification for every access request, regardless of the user's location or network. Implementing multifactor authentication, device authentication and continuous monitoring ensures that every access attempt undergoes rigorous scrutiny, reducing the success rate of social engineering attacks.

Security Incident Response Plan: Develop a comprehensive incident response plan that includes specific protocols for handling social engineering incidents. The plan should outline roles and responsibilities, communication channels, containment strategies and recovery procedures. Test the plan regularly through simulated exercises to ensure the organization can respond effectively to social engineering attacks.

Employee Reporting and Communication: Establish clear channels for employees to report suspicious activities and potential social engineering attempts. Encourage an open and non-punitive reporting culture, where employees feel safe reporting incidents without fear of retribution. Promptly communicate known social engineering threats or incidents to employees to raise awareness and help them stay vigilant.

External Communication Guidelines: Educate employees about the risks of sharing sensitive information with external parties, especially through phone calls, emails or social media. Emphasize the importance of verifying the identity of unknown individuals or organizations before disclosing any confidential data.

Regular Security Reviews: Conduct regular reviews of security policies, procedures and access controls to ensure they align with the evolving threat landscape and best practices. Involve key stakeholders from various departments to gather diverse perspectives and input.

Social engineering remains a formidable threat that continues to evolve alongside technology and human behavior. By understanding the psychological principles used by cybercriminals and they tactics organizations can build stronger defenses against social engineering attacks.

Continuous education and training are essential in keeping employees vigilant and prepared to identify and report potential social engineering attempts. Organizations must invest in robust cybersecurity solutions, such as user behavior analytics, AI driven monitoring and endpoint protection to detect and prevent social engineering attacks proactively.

XII. ANSWERS TO COMMON QUESTIONS

A. Overview

In this section, we will explain the reasons for the common cyber security measures that are frequently encountered in daily life and the answers to common questions.

B. Questions

B.1. Why You Should Physically Turn Off Your Laptop Camera?

Covering the camera of a laptop has become a common practice due to concerns about privacy and potential security risks. Here are the main reasons why users might consider covering their laptop cameras:

Privacy Protection: Hackers and malicious softwares can potentially gain unauthorized access to a laptop's camera. This could allow them to capture images and videos of you without your consent, invading your personal space and potentially compromising your privacy.

Preventing Remote Surveillance: Some sophisticated malwares or spywares can activate a laptop's camera without the user's knowledge or consent. Covering the camera physically prevents any unintended or unauthorized remote activation, making it difficult for anyone to spy on you through your camera.

Protection Against Vulnerability Exploitation: Cybercriminals may exploit vulnerabilities in software or hardware to gain access to your camera. Covering the camera is a simple precautionary step to mitigate this risk.

Ransomware Attacks: In some cases, cybercriminals may target individuals or organizations with ransomware attacks, where they threaten to release sensitive or compromising information unless a ransom is paid. Having your camera covered can prevent hackers from using potentially embarrassing or personal images as leverage.

Accidental Activation: Even without malicious intent, cameras can be accidentally activated during video conferences or other applications, potentially leading to embarrassing situations. Covering the camera ensures that you have control over when the camera is active.

Covering the camera is a good precaution but it's not a foolproof solution. The decision to cover your laptop's camera is a personal choice based on your own comfort level with the potential risks and your desire to maintain your privacy and security.

Also remember that covering the camera alone doesn't address potential concerns related to your laptop's microphone. Just as hackers might gain unauthorized access to your camera, they could also exploit vulnerabilities to access your microphone without your knowledge.

Here are some of the dangers associated with computer and mobile device microphones in terms of cybersecurity:

Unauthorized Access and Eavesdropping: Hackers could potentially gain unauthorized access to a device's microphone, allowing them to listen in on conversations, meetings and private discussions without the user's knowledge or consent. This invasive form of eavesdropping can lead to the exposure of personal and confidential information.

Voice Biometrics Exploitation: Voice biometrics used for authentication and verification purposes can be manipulated by sophisticated attackers. Voice recordings collected through compromised microphones might be used to gain unauthorized access to secure systems or accounts, circumventing voice-based security measures.

Audio Data Mining: Microphone enabled devices continuously collect audio data from their surroundings. This data can be exploited by third parties for audio data mining where speech patterns, keywords and emotional signs are analyzed to build detailed profiles of users, violating their privacy and potentially enabling targeted advertising or manipulation.

Data Leakage: Apps and software that have microphone access permissions can inadvertently or intentionally leak recorded audio data to unauthorized parties. This can happen due to vulnerabilities, insecure app design or even malicious intent on the part of app developers.

IoT Vulnerabilities: Internet of Things (IoT) devices often come equipped with microphones, might lack robust security measures due to their rushed development or minimal computing resources. This makes them attractive targets for attackers looking to compromise networks or gather information from multiple devices.

Unlike cameras, the microphone in a laptop or mobile device is integrated in a way that cannot be completely covered. Also, covering the microphone on mobile phones will not be an effective solution as it will prevent normal communication. To mitigate the dangers regarding microphones in computer and mobile devices, users should take some actions:

Manage Permissions: Regularly review and manage app permissions, especially microphone access. Only grant access to apps that genuinely require it and come from reputable sources.

Physical Security: When not in use, consider physically covering built-in microphones.

B.2. What is "Peer-to-Peer Encryption" for Mobile Messaging Apps?

Peer-to-peer encryption is a type of encryption where the data is encrypted on the sender's device and can only be decrypted by the recipient's device. This means that no one else (including the messaging app company itself) can read the messages.

Peer-to-peer encryption is extremely important for mobile messaging apps because it helps to protect users' privacy and security. With peer-to-peer encryption, users can be confident that their messages will not be intercepted or read by third parties. This is especially important for users who are sending sensitive information such as passwords, credit card numbers or financial records.

Peer-to-peer encryption also helps to protect users from cyber attacks. If hackers are able to compromise the messaging app company's servers, they will still not be able to read the messages because they will be encrypted.

B.3.   What is Multi-Factor Authentication (MFA)?

Multi-factor authentication (MFA) is a security measure that requires users to provide two or more factors of authentication to access an account or device. This makes it more difficult for attackers to gain unauthorized access, even if they have compromised one factor of authentication.

There are three main types of authentication factors:

Knowledge factors: Something you know such as a password, PIN or security question.

Possession factors: Something you have such as a smartphone or physical security key.

Biological factors: Something you are such as a fingerprint, facial scan or voiceprint.

MFA typically requires users to provide two factors from different categories. For example, you might need to enter your password (a knowledge factor) and scan your fingerprint (a biological factor) to log in to your bank account.

Here are some tips for enabling MFA:

Use different types of authentication factors for each account. This will make it more difficult for attackers to gain access to multiple accounts if they compromise one factor of authentication. Enable MFA for all of your important accounts such as your email, bank accounts and social media. Keep your authentication factors safe. For example, if you are using a security key for MFA, make sure to keep it in a safe place. Be aware of phishing attacks that attempt to trick you into revealing your MFA codes. Never reveal your MFA codes to anyone, even if they claim to be from a legitimate organization.

B.4. Why is it that when my phone is beside me, whenever I mention any product, its advertisement immediately appears on my phone or computer right after? Are devices listening us all the time?

That's a common question in these days. This situation is generally referred to as "targeted advertising" or "personalized advertising". Such ads are customized based on the user's interests and behaviors using various data collection and analysis methods. Here are some possible reasons for how this works:

Voice Recognition and Analysis: Smartphones and other devices can listen to sounds in the background. Additionally some apps or services can detect specific keywords or terms by processing user conversations. For example, when you mention a product name, they can detect this keyword and target relevant ads.

Location and Contextual Information: Your phone can determine your location using features like GPS and wi-fi. Location information can be used to present relevant ads when you enter a specific store or are in a particular area.

Browser History and App Usage: The history of apps you use and your browser can reflect your interests and shopping behavior. This data can help advertisers offer you more suitable product or service recommendations.

Social Media and Online Interactions: Social media platforms and other online services can perform data analysis to target ads based on user behavior. For instance, your likes, shares and followed accounts on social media can be used to identify your interests. There is a modern proverb on this: "If the service is free, you're the product."

Cookies and Tracking Technologies: Browser cookies and similar tracking technologies can monitor your online activities and share this information with advertisers. This way ads can be customized based on your behaviors across different websites and apps.

These processes usually occur with the user's permission or consent. Advertisers generally work to protect user privacy and be transparent about data collection in accordance with policies and legal requirements. In most cases, the foundation of targeted advertising lies in user consent.

If targeted advertising raises concerns about your personal privacy, it's important to review and customize the privacy settings of your devices and apps.

Targeted advertising and personalized content delivery are closely related to concepts like data mining and big data. Those are similar but different terms.

Data Mining: Data mining involves the process of discovering patterns, trends and insights from large sets of data. In the context of targeted advertising, data mining techniques are used to analyze vast amounts of user data to identify patterns in user behavior, preferences and interactions. This information is then used to tailor advertisements and content to individual users, increasing the likelihood of engagement and conversion.

Big Data: Big data refers to the massive volume of structured and unstructured data that organizations collect and process. In the case of targeted advertising, big data includes a wide range of information such as user demographics, browsing history, app usage, social media interactions, location data and more. This extensive data collection provides a rich source of information for advertisers to understand user preferences and deliver personalized experiences.

Personalization and Targeting: The combination of data mining and big data enables companies to create highly personalized experiences for users. By analyzing large datasets and identifying patterns, companies can segment users into specific groups based on shared characteristics. This segmentation allows them to tailor advertisements, recommendations and content to individual users interests and preferences, resulting in more effective marketing efforts.

Machine Learning and AI: Advanced data mining and big data analytics often involve machine learning and artificial intelligence techniques. These technologies can automate the process of analyzing data, identifying patterns and predicting user behavior. Machine learning algorithms can continuously refine their understanding of user preferences, leading to increasingly accurate and relevant personalized recommendations and ads.

In essence, targeted advertising and personalized content delivery leverage data mining and big data analytics to optimize the effectiveness of marketing efforts. This involves collecting, processing and interpreting large amounts of user data to create customized experiences that resonate with individual users.

Future Impacts and Implications

This is a subject that falls outside the scope of the main theme of the book but it still needs to be mentioned.

Data mining and the use of big data can have both positive and negative impacts on society. While they offer many benefits in terms of improving services and personalization, they also raise concerns about privacy, security and potential misuse. Here are some potential dangers and future impacts of data mining and big data, including their malicious use:

Privacy Invasion and Surveillance:

Data Aggregation: Data mining involves the aggregation of disparate data sources, which, when combined, can reveal intricate details about individuals' private lives, habits and preferences.

Third-party Data Sharing: Data brokers and third-party companies often collect and sell personal data, leading to the widespread sharing of personal information without individuals' explicit consent.

Location Tracking: Mobile devices' location data can provide insights into an individual's movements, habits and daily routines when analyzed.

Social Engineering:

Psychographic Profiling: Data mining can create psychographic profiles that predict individual behavior, allowing attackers to craft convincing messages that exploit psychological vulnerabilities.

Identity Mimicry: Detailed personal information can be used to convincingly impersonate individuals in scams or fraudulent activities.

Political Manipulation and Election Fraud:

Microtargeting: Political campaigns can use data-driven microtargeting to identify and reach specific demographics with tailored messages, potentially swaying public opinion.

Fake News Amplification: Mined data can identify audiences vulnerable to disinformation, amplifying the spread of fake news and divisive content.

Voter Suppression: Malicious actors could use voter data to create fake voter registration sites or spread misinformation about election procedures to suppress voter turnout.

Surveillance Capitalism:

Predictive Analytics: Companies leverage big data and machine learning to predict consumer behavior, optimizing marketing strategies to increase sales.

Filter Bubbles: Algorithms use personal data to serve content that aligns with users existing beliefs, reinforcing echo chambers and limiting exposure to diverse viewpoints.

Discrimination and Bias:

Algorithmic Bias: Algorithms trained on historical data can perpetuate societal biases, leading to discriminatory outcomes in critical areas like lending, hiring and criminal justice.

Redlining 2.0: Predictive analytics can inadvertently reinforce discriminatory practices, creating a digital form of redlining by unfairly denying opportunities to marginalized groups. (Redlining refers to a discriminatory practice that emerged in the United States in the early to mid-20th century, primarily during the 1930s to the 1960s. It was a systematic way of denying loans, insurance or other financial services to specific neighborhoods or communities based on their racial or ethnic composition)

Loss of Personal Agency:

Nudge Theory: Behavioral insights from data mining can be used to subtly influence individuals decisions, leading to concerns about manipulation of personal choices. (At its core, nudge theory recognizes that human decision-making is often subject to cognitive biases and heuristics that can lead to less-than-optimal outcomes. By understanding these biases, policymakers and organizations can design choice architectures that facilitate better decision-making. These interventions are designed to harness the predictably irrational aspects of human behavior and encourage choices that promote personal health, financial stability, environmental conservation and more)

Surveillance Capitalism's Influence: The continuous monitoring of behaviors can lead to the commodification of personal experiences, undermining genuine connections and personal autonomy.

Orwellian Surveillance State:

Mass Surveillance: The convergence of data from various sources, including social media, internet browsing and IoT devices could enable governments or corporations to conduct mass surveillance similar to the dystopian world depicted in George Orwell's "1984" novel.

Predictive Policing: Law enforcement agencies could use predictive analytics to preemptively identify potential criminals, raising concerns about due process and individual rights.

Striking a balance between the potential benefits and risks of data mining and big data requires careful consideration of technological advancements, ethical principles and legal frameworks to ensure a future where data driven innovation is harnessed responsibly for the improvement of society. This is actually one of the most important topics about the future of cybersecurity.

B.5.　　What is Digital Footprint?

Our online presence leaves a trail of data that collectively forms our digital footprint. This footprint encompasses the digital breadcrumbs we unwittingly scatter across various platforms and interactions, providing valuable insights into our lives, preferences and behaviors. Understanding the implications of our digital footprint is important for safeguarding our privacy. In this chapter, we will examine the concept of the digital footprint, exploring its significance, potential risks and measures to mitigate its impact.

Defining the Digital Footprint

Every digital engagement from social media interactions to online shopping behaviors, contributes to the growing pool of information that constitutes our digital footprint. Data collection from digital footprint can occur through both active and passive means. Active data collection involves willingly sharing information on social media, filling out online forms or posting updates. In contrast, passive data collection occurs behind the scenes, where various entities track and gather data without explicit user consent, often for marketing or analytical purposes.

The Significance of Digital Footprints

Digital footprints provide valuable data for businesses and organizations to analyze user behavior, trends and demographics.

This information helps them refine products, services and marketing strategies to better cater to their target audience.

The digital footprint plays an important role in shaping our online reputation. Information shared publicly or leaked accidentally can have unimaginable consequences on personal and professional relationships.

Risks Associated with Digital Footprints

Identity Theft and Fraud: One of the most significant risks associated with a digital footprint is identity theft. Malicious actors can exploit publicly available information to piece together details necessary for committing identity fraud.

Social Engineering Attacks: Cybercriminals often use information gathered from digital footprints to craft convincing social engineering attacks, manipulating individuals into revealing sensitive information or performing malicious actions.

Data Breaches and Privacy Violations: Inadequate data protection measures can lead to data breaches, resulting in the exposure of sensitive information and potential privacy violations.

Minimizing Your Digital Footprint

Privacy Settings and Permissions: Review and adjust privacy settings on social media platforms, online services and apps to control the information you share and limit access to your data.

Responsible Social Media Use: Be cautious about the information you post on social media, particularly regarding personal details and location information. Think twice before sharing sensitive content that may come back to haunt you.

Limiting Third-Party Access: Be mindful of granting permissions to third-party apps and services that request access to your data. Limit such access to only essential functionalities.

Regular Data Audits: Conduct periodic audits of your digital footprint to identify and remove outdated or unnecessary information, reducing the exposure of potentially sensitive data.

Digital Footprint and Professional Life

Job Hunting and Social Media Screening: Employers often perform social media screenings of potential candidates. Ensure that your digital footprint portrays a professional and positive image.

Online Branding and Networking: Your digital footprint can be a powerful tool for personal branding and networking. Engage thoughtfully and responsibly to build a reputable online presence.

Understanding your digital footprint is crucial where data is the currency of the digital realm. Your online activities leave traces that can shape your experiences, privacy and security. Remember, every digital step you take contributes to the ever expanding tapestry of your digital presence. So tread mindfully and responsibly in the digital world.

XIII. THE FUTURE OF CYBERSECURITY

Drifting the endless space of online world, almost every aspect of our lives now relies on digital systems. However, this exponential growth in technology also brings forth new and complex cybersecurity challenges. As we step into the future, the landscape of cybersecurity is set to evolve in unprecedented ways, demanding innovative strategies to protect against emerging threats.

A. Artificial Intelligence (AI) and Machine Learning (ML)

One of the most significant trends in internet security is the increased use of artificial intelligence (AI) and machine learning (ML) in security solutions. AI and ML algorithms are already being used to detect and respond to cyber threats more quickly and accurately than traditional methods. In the future, we can expect to see even more advanced uses of AI and ML in internet security, such as predictive threat intelligence and real-time threat analysis.

Cyber threats come in various forms, ranging from phishing attacks and ransomware to sophisticated Advanced Persistent Threats (APT). These threats exploit vulnerabilities in networks, software and human behavior, posing significant risks to sensitive data, critical infrastructure and individual privacy. Traditional cybersecurity measures are often not enough to combat these rapidly evolving threats.

A.1.   Artificial Intelligence in Cybersecurity

Artificial intelligence is the science and engineering of creating machines or systems that can perform tasks that normally require human intelligence such as learning, reasoning, decision making and problem solving. AI can be applied to various domains and industries.

Artificial intelligence in cybersecurity is the use of AI techniques and tools to enhance the security and resilience of information systems and networks. AI can help cybersecurity professionals to automate and optimize various tasks and processes such as data analysis, threat detection or user authentication. AI can also help cybersecurity researchers to discover and mitigate new and emerging cyber threats.

However, artificial intelligence in cybersecurity also poses some challenges and risks that need to be addressed. AI can also be used by cyber attackers to launch more sophisticated and stealthy attacks such as adversarial machine learning or botnet attacks. AI can also introduce new vulnerabilities or biases in the security systems or algorithms that can be exploited or manipulated by malicious actors. AI can also raise ethical or legal issues regarding the privacy.

Applications and Benefits of Artificial Intelligence in Cybersecurity

Artificial intelligence in cybersecurity can be applied to various domains and functions, such as:

Data analysis: AI can help cybersecurity professionals to collect, process, analyze and visualize large amounts of data from various sources, such as logs, alerts, reports or sensors. AI can use techniques such as natural language processing (NLP), computer vision (CV) or data mining (DM) to extract useful information and insights from the data. AI can also use techniques such as machine learning (ML), deep learning (DL) or neural networks (NN) to learn from the data and identify patterns or anomalies. AI can help cybersecurity professionals to gain a better understanding of the security situation and make informed decisions.

Threat detection: AI can help cybersecurity professionals to detect and identify various types of cyber threats, such as malware, ransomware, phishing or denial-of-service attacks. AI can use techniques such as signature-based detection, behavior-based detection or anomaly-based detection to compare the observed activity with the known or expected activity and flag any deviations or suspicious events. AI can also use techniques such as supervised learning, unsupervised learning or reinforcement learning to learn from the historical or real-time data and discover new or unknown threats. AI can help cybersecurity professionals to reduce the false positives or false negatives and increase the accuracy and speed of threat detection.

Incident response: AI can help cybersecurity professionals to respond to and recover from cyber incidents, such as breaches, attacks or intrusions. AI can use techniques such as automated reasoning, planning or decision making to generate the optimal response strategy or action plan based on the severity, impact or context of the incident. AI can also use techniques such as automation orchestration or collaboration to execute the response actions or tasks with minimal human intervention or supervision. AI can help cybersecurity professionals to mitigate the damage or loss and restore the normal operation of the system or network.

Risk assessment: AI can help cybersecurity professionals to assess and manage the security risks associated with their information systems or networks. AI can use techniques such as probabilistic reasoning, fuzzy logic or game theory to estimate the likelihood, consequence or cost of potential threats or vulnerabilities. AI can also use techniques such as optimization, simulation or scenario analysis to evaluate the effectiveness, efficiency or trade-offs of different security measures or controls. AI can help cybersecurity professionals to prioritize the most critical or urgent risks and allocate the appropriate resources or budget to address them.

A.2.   Machine Learning in Cybersecurity

Machine Learning is a subset of AI that empowers systems to learn from data and improve their performance without being explicitly programmed. ML algorithms can analyze historical cyber incident data and identify trends, thereby enabling the prediction of potential threats. By continuously learning from new data, ML models adapt to emerging threats, enhancing the overall effectiveness of cyber defense.

A.3.   Behavioral Analytics

AI-driven behavioral analytics is a game-changer in cyber defense. By studying user behavior and establishing patterns of normal activity, AI systems can swiftly detect deviations that might indicate potential threats, such as insider attacks or compromised accounts. Behavioral analytics complement traditional signature-based approaches, enhancing the overall security posture.

A.4.   Malware Detection and Prevention

Malware poses a severe threat to computer systems and networks. AI and ML algorithms have significantly improved malware detection and prevention techniques. ML models can identify and classify malware based on its characteristics, enabling real-time protection against both known and zero-day threats.

A.5.   Adaptive Authentication

Authentication is a critical aspect of cybersecurity and AI has a significant role in making it more robust. Adaptive authentication uses AI to assess the risk associated with each authentication attempt. Based on various factors such as location, device and user behavior, AI can determine the level of authentication required, offering a seamless user experience while maintaining security.

A.6.   Threat Hunting

Traditional cybersecurity methods often focus on reactive measures, waiting for threats to surface before addressing them. AI-enabled threat hunting reverses this approach. By employing ML algorithms to sift through vast amounts of data, cybersecurity professionals can proactively identify potential threats and take preemptive action.

A.7.   Incident Response and Recovery

When a cyber incident occurs, swift and effective response is crucial. AI and ML can significantly improve incident response times by automating the analysis of incident data, classifying the severity of the threat and suggesting appropriate remediation measures.

A.8.   Challenges and Limitations

While AI and ML offer immense potential for cyber defense, they also come with challenges. Training AI models requires extensive and diverse data sets, which may be challenging to obtain. Additionally, adversarial attacks seek to exploit vulnerabilities in AI systems. Continuous monitoring and updating of AI models are essential to address these concerns.

B. Internet of Things (IoT) Security

The internet of things (IoT) has been growing rapidly in recent years and with this growth comes increased security risks. As more devices become connected to the internet, it becomes easier for attackers to gain access to sensitive information. Future trends in internet security will focus on improving IoT security to protect against these threats, including the development of secure IoT protocols, better device authentication and access control methods and the use of secure communication protocols such as MQTT or CoAP.

C. Blockchain and Cryptocurrency Security

Blockchain and cryptocurrency are two of the most disruptive and innovative technologies in the field of cybersecurity. Blockchain is a distributed ledger technology that records transactions in a secure and transparent way. Cryptocurrency is a digital asset that uses blockchain as its underlying platform to enable peer-to-peer exchange of value without intermediaries.

Blockchain and cryptocurrency offer many benefits for cybersecurity, such as:

Decentralization: Blockchain and cryptocurrency operate on a network of nodes that share the responsibility of validating transactions and maintaining the ledger. This eliminates the need for centralized authorities or trusted third parties that can be compromised or corrupted.

Encryption: Blockchain and cryptocurrency use cryptographic techniques such as hashing, digital signatures and public-key cryptography, to protect the data and the identity of the participants. This ensures the confidentiality, integrity and authenticity of the transactions and the ledger.

Consensus: Blockchain and cryptocurrency use various algorithms, such as proof-of-work, proof-of-stake or proof-of-authority, to achieve agreement among the nodes on the state of the ledger. This prevents double-spending or manipulation of the data.

Transparency: Blockchain and cryptocurrency provide a public and verifiable record of all transactions that can be audited and traced by anyone. This enhances the accountability and trustworthiness of the system.

However, blockchain and cryptocurrency also face some challenges and limitations that need to be addressed. Some of these challenges are:

Scalability: Blockchain and cryptocurrency have difficulty in handling large volumes of transactions or data due to their inherent design. This affects their performance and and usability.

Privacy: Blockchain and cryptocurrency expose some information about the transactions and the participants to the public such as the amount, the address and the timestamp. This may compromise the privacy or anonymity of the users or reveal sensitive data.

Regulation: Blockchain and cryptocurrency operate in a largely unregulated or unclear legal environment that may pose risks or uncertainties for the users or the stakeholders. This may affect their liability.

Security: Blockchain and cryptocurrency are not immune to cyberattacks or vulnerabilities that may exploit their weaknesses or flaws. This may result in loss of the assets.

Types of Threats

Threats can be classified into two categories: external attacks or internal attacks. External attacks are those that originate from outside sources that try to breach or disrupt the system. Internal attacks are those that originate from inside sources that try to manipulate the system.

Some examples of external attacks are:

Denial-of-service (DoS) attacks: DoS attacks are those that aim to overload or overwhelm the network or the nodes with malicious traffic or requests. This can slow down or interrupt the normal functioning of the system or prevent legitimate users from accessing it.

Sybil attacks: Sybil attacks are those that create multiple fake identities or nodes on the network to gain influence or control over it. This can affect the consensus mechanism, the reputation system or the voting process of the system.

Eclipse attacks: Eclipse attacks are those that isolate a node or a group of nodes from the rest of the network by intercepting or blocking their communication channels. This can create a false view of the ledger or the transactions for the affected nodes or cause them to miss important updates or events.

51% attacks: 51% attacks are those that gain more than half of the computing power or the stake on the network to manipulate the ledger or the transactions. This can allow them to reverse or alter previous transactions, double-spend their coins or prevent new transactions from being confirmed.

Some examples of internal attacks are:

Double-spending attacks: Double-spending attacks are those that try to spend the same coins twice by creating conflicting transactions or forks on the ledger. This can defraud the recipients or undermine the value of the currency.

Selfish mining attacks: Selfish mining attacks are those that try to gain an unfair advantage over other miners by hiding their mined blocks from the network until they have a longer chain than the public chain. This can allow them to claim more rewards, waste other miners' resources or cause forks on the ledger.

Bribery attacks: Bribery attacks are those that try to influence the behavior of other participants by offering them incentives or rewards for acting in a certain way. This can affect the consensus mechanism, the voting process or the security protocol of the system.

D. Cloud Security

Cloud computing has become an essential tool for organizations of all sizes and cloud security will continue to be a significant trend in internet security. As organizations rely more on cloud services for their digital operations, the need for effective cloud security solutions will become even more critical. Future trends in cloud security will focus on improving data privacy and security, such as the use of secure cloud storage, the development of secure cloud-based applications and the implementation of multi-factor authentication for cloud services.

E. Biometric Authentication and Zero Trust Architecture

Biometric authentication is the process of verifying the identity of a person based on their physical or behavioral characteristics such as fingerprint, face, iris, voice or keystroke dynamics. Biometric authentication offers several advantages over traditional methods of authentication such as passwords or PINs which can be forgotten or compromised. Biometric authentication is more convenient and secure as it relies on the inherent features of the person that are hard to imitate.

Zero trust architecture is a security model that assumes that no entity (user, device, network or resource) can be trusted by default and requires continuous verification before granting access. Zero trust architecture follows the principle of "never trust, always verify" and implements dynamic policies that enforce the least-privilege principle. Zero trust architecture aims to prevent unauthorized access and data breaches.

Biometric authentication and zero trust architecture are complementary technologies that can enhance the security and usability of access control systems. Biometric authentication can provide strong and continuous verification of the identity and context of the user, while zero trust architecture can enforce strict and adaptive policies based on the risk level of the user and the resource. Together, biometric authentication and zero trust architecture can provide a high level of assurance and protection for sensitive data and applications.

Biometric Authentication Technologies

Biometric authentication technologies can be classified into two categories: physiological biometrics and behavioral biometrics. Physiological biometrics are based on the physical traits of the person such as fingerprint, face or retina. Behavioral biometrics are based on the actions or patterns of the person such as voice, signature or gesture.

Physiological biometrics are usually more stable and consistent than behavioral biometrics but they may also be more intrusive and vulnerable to spoofing attacks. Behavioral biometrics are usually more dynamic and variable than physiological biometrics, but they may also be more user-friendly and resilient to spoofing attacks. Both types of biometrics have their own strengths and weaknesses and they can be combined to achieve higher performance and security.

Some examples of biometric authentication technologies are:

Fingerprint recognition: Fingerprint recognition is one of the most widely used and accepted biometric technologies. It is based on the unique pattern of ridges and valleys on the surface of the finger. Fingerprint recognition can be performed by capturing an image of the finger using an optical or capacitive sensor and comparing it with a stored template using various algorithms. Fingerprint recognition is fast, accurate and convenient but it may also be affected by dirt, moisture or wear on the finger.

Face recognition: Face recognition is based on the distinctive features of the face. It can be performed by capturing an image or a video of the face using a camera and comparing it with a stored template using various algorithms. Face recognition is user-friendly, non-intrusive and widely available but it may also be influenced by lighting, pose, expression, makeup or accessories.

Iris recognition: Iris recognition is based on the unique pattern of the iris, the colored ring around the pupil of the eye. Iris recognition can be performed by capturing an image of the eye using an infrared camera and comparing it with a stored template using various algorithms. Iris recognition is very accurate and secure but it may also be expensive and sensitive to eye conditions or contact lenses.

Voice recognition: Voice recognition is based on the distinctive features of the voice. It can be performed by capturing an audio sample of the voice and comparing it with a stored template using various algorithms. Voice recognition is widely available but it may also be affected by noise, illness or accent.

Keystroke dynamics: Keystroke dynamics is based on the unique way of typing on a keyboard such as the speed, pressure, rhythm or duration of each keystroke. It can be performed by capturing the keystroke data using a software application and comparing it with a stored template using various algorithms. Keystroke dynamics is low-cost and easy to implement but it may also be influenced by typing style or device.

Zero Trust Architecture Principles

Zero trust architecture is a security model that challenges the traditional perimeter-based approach that assumes that everything inside the network is trusted and everything outside the network is untrusted. Zero trust architecture adopts a data-centric and identity-driven approach that assumes that nothing can be trusted by default and everything must be verified before granting access.

Zero trust architecture follows these core principles:

Verify explicitly: Every request for access must be authenticated, authorized and encrypted, regardless of the source or location. No implicit trust is granted based on network parameters such as IP or MAC address. Verification is based on multiple factors such as identity, device or context.

Use least-privilege access: Every user and device must be granted the minimum amount of access required to perform their function and no more. Access is granted on a need-to-know and need-to-use basis and is revoked when no longer needed. Access is also limited in time and scope and is subject to continuous review and audit.

Assume breach: Every user and device must be treated as a potential threat and monitored for anomalous or malicious behavior. Any sign of compromise must be detected and isolated as soon as possible. Security controls must be applied at every layer and every stage of the data lifecycle.

Microsegment the network: The network must be divided into small and isolated segments that have their own security policies and controls. Each segment must have a clear boundary and a defined purpose. Communication between segments must be restricted and regulated. This reduces the attack surface and prevents the lateral movement of attackers within the network.

Embrace automation and orchestration: The security policies and controls must be automated and orchestrated using software defined tools and techniques. This enables faster and more consistent enforcement of the policies and controls across the network. It also enables real time adaptation of the policies and controls based on the changing threat landscape and business requirements.

Biometric Authentication in Support of Zero Trust Architecture

Biometric authentication can support zero trust architecture by providing strong and continuous verification of the identity and context of the user. Biometric authentication can enhance the security and usability of access control systems in the following ways:

Biometric authentication can provide a higher level of assurance than password based authentication as it relies on the inherent features of the user that are hard to imitate. Biometric authentication can prevent common attacks such as phishing, credential stuffing or password cracking.

It can provide a more convenient and user friendly experience than password based authentication as it eliminates the need to remember passwords. Biometric authentication can improve user satisfaction and productivity.

It can provide a more dynamic and adaptive verification than password based authentication as it can capture the changes in the user's behavior or context over time. Biometric authentication can enable risk based authentication which adjusts the level of verification based on the level of risk associated with the user or the resource.

It can also provide a more continuous verification than password based authentication as it can monitor the user's activity or presence throughout the session. Biometric authentication can enable continuous authentication which verifies the user's identity at regular intervals or at critical events.

Challenges and Best Practices for Biometric Authentication

Biometric authentication is not a silver bullet for security and it also faces some challenges and limitations that need to be addressed. Some of these challenges are:

Privacy: Biometric data is sensitive personal data that may reveal information about the user's identity, health, ethnicity or preferences. Biometric data must be collected, stored, processed and transmitted with the user's consent and in compliance with the relevant laws and regulations. Biometric data must also be protected from unauthorized access, disclosure or misuse by the service provider or third parties.

Accuracy: Biometric systems are not perfect and may produce errors in matching the biometric data with the stored template. These errors may result in false positives (accepting an impostor) or false negatives (rejecting a legitimate user). Biometric systems must be calibrated and tested to achieve optimal performance and minimize errors.

Spoofing: Biometric systems may be vulnerable to spoofing attacks where an attacker tries to fool the system by presenting a fake biometric sample such as a fake fingerprint, photo, video or a voice recording. Biometric systems must implement anti spoofing techniques such as liveness detection to prevent spoofing attacks.

User acceptance: Biometric systems may face resistance from some users who may perceive them as intrusive or unreliable. Biometric systems must ensure user acceptance by providing clear information, education and feedback about the benefits, risks and options of biometric authentication. Biometric systems must also allow user choice and control over their biometric data.

Some best practices for biometric authentication are:

Use biometrics as a part of a multi-factor authentication scheme, where biometrics is combined with another factor such as a password or a code. This can provide an additional layer of security and mitigate the impact of biometric errors or spoofing.

Use biometrics as a part of a zero trust architecture, where biometrics is integrated with other security components such as identity and access management, network segmentation, data encryption or threat detection. This can provide an adaptive security solution that can protect the data from attacks.

F. Quantum Computing and Post-Quantum Cryptography

Quantum computing is a rapidly evolving field that promises to revolutionize many areas of science and technology such as artificial intelligence, cryptography, optimization, simulation and machine learning. However, quantum computing also poses a serious threat to the security of current cryptographic systems that are widely used to protect the confidentiality, integrity and authenticity of information.

What is quantum computing?

Quantum computing is a paradigm of computation that relies on the principles of quantum mechanics, such as superposition, entanglement and interference. Unlike classical computers that use bits (binary digits) that can only be in one of two states (0 or 1), quantum computers use qubits (quantum bits) that can be in a superposition of both states at the same time. This means that a qubit can represent both 0 and 1 with some probability until it is measured and collapses to a definite state.

Moreover, qubits can be entangled with each other, meaning that their states are correlated even when they are physically separated. This allows quantum computers to perform parallel operations on multiple qubits simultaneously, exploiting quantum interference to amplify the probability of the desired outcome and cancel out the undesired ones. As a result, quantum computers can potentially solve some problems much faster than classical computers, especially those that involve finding patterns or factors in large data sets.

How can quantum computing break cryptography?

Cryptography relies on two types of algorithms: symmetric-key algorithms and public-key algorithms. Symmetric-key algorithms use the same secret key for both encryption and decryption while public-key algorithms use different keys for encryption and decryption, where one key is public and the other is private.

The security of symmetric-key algorithms depends on the difficulty of finding the secret key by brute force, i.e. trying all possible keys until finding the correct one. The security of public-key algorithms depends on the difficulty of solving certain mathematical problems that are easy to perform in one direction but hard to reverse such as finding the prime factors of a large number or finding the discrete logarithm of a number in a finite field. These problems are known as hard problems or trapdoor functions.

Quantum computing can break some of the most popular cryptographic algorithms by using special quantum algorithms that can solve these hard problems much faster than classical algorithms. The most famous quantum algorithm is Shor's algorithm, which can factor large numbers and find discrete logarithms in polynomial time, i.e. in time proportional to some power of the size of the input. This means that Shor's algorithm can break public-key algorithms such as RSA, Diffie-Hellman and Elliptic Curve Cryptography, which are widely used for key exchange and digital signatures.

Another quantum algorithm that can threaten cryptography is Grover's algorithm, which can find an element in an unsorted database or a solution to a Boolean function in square root time, i.e. in time proportional to the square root of the size of the input. This means that Grover's algorithm can speed up brute force attacks against symmetric-key algorithms such as AES and SHA-2 which are widely used for encryption and hashing.

What are the possible solutions to mitigate this threat?

The threat posed by quantum computing to cryptography has motivated researchers to develop new cryptographic algorithms that are resistant to quantum attacks. These algorithms are collectively known as post-quantum cryptography or quantum-resistant cryptography. Post-quantum cryptography is based on mathematical problems that are believed to be hard for both classical and quantum computers such as lattice problems, multivariate problems, code-based problems or hash-based problems.

Post-quantum cryptography aims to provide equivalent or better security than current cryptographic algorithms, while maintaining reasonable efficiency and compatibility with existing systems. However, post-quantum cryptography is still an active area of research and many challenges remain to be solved before it can be widely adopted. Some of these challenges include:

- Proving the security and hardness of post-quantum algorithms under realistic assumptions and models.
- Evaluating the performance and scalability of post-quantum algorithms in terms of speed, memory, bandwidth and power consumption.
- Developing standards and protocols for post-quantum algorithms that ensure interoperability and compliance with existing systems.
- Testing and validating post-quantum algorithms against potential attacks and vulnerabilities.

- Educating and raising awareness among users and stakeholders about the need and benefits of post-quantum cryptography.

Quantum computing is a double-edged sword for cybersecurity. It can offer new opportunities for enhancing security and privacy but it can also pose a serious threat to the security of current cryptographic systems. Therefore, it's essential to prepare for the advent of quantum computing by developing and deploying post-quantum cryptography, which can ensure the long-term security of information in the quantum era.

CONCLUSION

We've explored various aspects of cybersecurity and the steps you can take to protect your information and systems from attacks. In conclusion, i hope that this book has given you a clear understanding of the various aspects of cybersecurity and the steps you can take to protect your information and systems from attacks. Whether you're an individual or a business, it's important to be aware of the threats you may face and to take the necessary steps to secure your information. You'll be better equipped to defend against cyber attacks and to respond effectively to security incidents by understanding the key concepts and topics in this book.

Final Thoughts and Recommendations for Improving Internet Security

The internet is a vast and constantly evolving landscape that offers tremendous opportunities for communication, commerce and information exchange. However, it also poses significant security challenges that require constant vigilance, attention and action. In this book, we have explored the many facets of internet security. As we have seen, the threats to internet security are many and diverse, ranging from phishing attacks and malware infections to data breaches and unauthorized access. These threats can have devastating consequences, including the loss of sensitive information, the theft of intellectual property or the disruption of critical systems and services.

To mitigate these risks, it is essential to adopt a multi-layered approach to internet security that includes a combination of technical organizational and educational measures. Technical measures include the deployment of security software and hardware, the implementation of security protocols and standards and the regular updating and patching of systems and software. Organizational measures include the development of security policies and procedures, the conduct of regular security audits and assessments and the deployment of trained security personnel. Educational measures include the training of employees and users on the importance of security and the recognition of security threats, as well as the provision of security awareness programs and training.

In addition to these measures, it is important to stay informed about the latest developments in internet security and to adopt best practices and emerging technologies as they become available. This may include the adoption of cloud-based security solutions, the use of mobile device management tools, the deployment of security information and event management systems and the implementation of blockchain-based solutions.

Another important aspect of improving internet security is to cultivate a culture of security within organizations and among users. This means fostering a shared understanding of the importance of security and a commitment to the protection of sensitive information and critical systems. It also means encouraging active involvement in security initiatives and programs, as well as a willingness to report security incidents and participate in incident response efforts.

The protection of internet security requires ongoing effort and attention, as well as the active participation of all stakeholders. By following best practices, staying informed and adopting a multi-layered approach organizations and users can greatly reduce the risks associated with the use of the internet and ensure the protection of sensitive information and critical systems.

I hope that this book has been informative and useful in helping you to understand the many aspects of internet security and the steps you can take to protect your systems and data. Thank you for reading.

Suggestions for Further Reading and Additional Resources on Cyber Security

There is a wealth of information available on internet security. Whether you are looking to deepen your understanding or simply get started in the field, there is something for everyone. I'll take a look at some suggestions for further reading and additional resources that will help you expand your knowledge of internet security.

Books

"Computer Security Fundamentals" by Chuck Easttom

This comprehensive guide provides a strong foundation in computer security, including key concepts, technologies and best practices. It is ideal for anyone who wants to understand the fundamentals of computer security, from students to professionals.

"Cryptography Engineering: Design Principles and Practical Applications" by Niels Ferguson, Bruce Schneier and Tadayoshi Kohno

This book provides an in-depth look at cryptography, covering everything from the basics to the most advanced concepts. Whether you're an experienced cryptography professional or just starting out, this book is an excellent resource.

"Incident Response & Computer Forensics" by Chris Prosise, Kevin Mandia, Matt Pepe and Andrew Whitaker

This book is a comprehensive guide to incident response and computer forensics and provides practical advice on how to prepare for and respond to security incidents. It is an ideal resource for security professionals and IT managers who want to be prepared for the worst.

Online Resources

SANS Institute

The SANS Institute is a leading provider of information security training, certifications and research. They offer a wide range of online resources, including articles, whitepapers and webinars, that provide in-depth information on a variety of security topics.

OWASP (Open Web Application Security Project)

OWASP is a non-profit organization dedicated to improving the security of software. They provide a wealth of information, including research, best practices and tools, to help organizations improve their security posture.

US-CERT (United States Computer Emergency Readiness Team): US-CERT is a division of the Department of Homeland Security and provides alerts, bulletins and other resources to help organizations respond to cyber threats.

www.ingramcontent.com/pod-product-compliance
Lightning Source LLC
Chambersburg PA
CBHW071104050326
40690CB00008B/1116